Making Disciples in the Congregation

A guide to
Christian formation
through the process
of mentoring and
the experience of
congregational worship

by Paul Versluis III
Foreword by Ross T. Bender

WIPF & STOCK · Eugene, Oregon

Wipf and Stock Publishers
199 W 8th Ave, Suite 3
Eugene, OR 97401

Making Disciples in the Congregation
A Guide to Christian Formation through the Process
of Mentoring and the Experience of Congregational Worship
By Versluis, Paul, III
Copyright©1995 Institute of Mennonite Studies
ISBN 13: 978-1-5326-1941-0
Publication date 3/24/2017
Previously published by Institute of Mennonite Studies, 1995

First published by Institute of Mennonite Studies (1995)

TABLE OF CONTENTS

ACKNOWLEDGMENTS

I am grateful to God whose grace was sufficient to enable me to undertake and complete this project. To the D. Min. class of 1989-90, especially to Rev. Douglas Pride and Rev. Douglas Slater, thank you for your friendship. To Dr. Andrew Purves and Dr. Marcus Smucker, thank you for your affirmation and your love for Jesus Christ. To the Maple Grove Mennonite Church in New Wilmington Pa., thank you for a place of peace and love. To the Foundation Mennonite Church in Erie Pa., thank you for your affirmation and your willingness to participate in this project. To those friends involved in the Research Seminar on Christian Initiation, I am grateful for shared wisdom. To Richard Herbold who taught me to use Word Perfect, thank you for serving me so graciously. To Dr. Terry Giles, thank you for the words, "Just get the crazy thing done". To Dr. Robert Hostetler who so often took my "pearls" and provided a "string", without your support and direction this project would be incomplete. To my family, Anna, Bethany, Sara, Rachel, Paul, and my wife Joy, thank you for a spirit of peace, love and joy. I am so blessed. To my mother and father, thank you for your compassion, your support, and your faith in Jesus Christ.

Paul Versluis III
March, 1994

FOREWORD

In June of 1992 and 1993, the Institute of Mennonite Studies in cooperation with the Mennonite Board of Congregational Ministries (Elkhart, Indiana), the General Conference Mennonite Commission on Education (Newton, Kansas) and the Congregational Literature Division of the Mennonite Publishing House (Scottdale, Pennsylvania) sponsored two sessions known as the Research Seminar on Christian Initiation (RSCI). The term "initiation" has to do with helping persons begin the Christian life and prepare for baptism and church membership. It is a term which is coming into popular usage as a result of the program developed in recent years by the Roman Catholic Church called Rites for the Christian Initiation of Adults (RCIA).

With the increasing emphasis of the Mennonite Church and the General Conference Mennonite Church on evangelism and church planting, there are a growing number of adult persons from various Christian traditions or no church backgrounds coming to our churches to seek membership. Pastors are calling for materials which will be helpful in adequately preparing these persons for meaningful membership in the congregation. Existing materials are primarily geared toward youth who have grown up in Christian families in our congregations. There are no instructional materials designed specifically for this new group of potential church members who bring a different set of questions in their search to begin the Christian life in a Mennonite perspective.

This is, in some ways, parallel to the situation of the early Christians in the second half of the first century and in the second century. As Jewish believers came for baptism and membership in the newly forming Christian church, they brought with them a Jewish faith and high moral standards. What they needed primarily was a reinterpretation of their faith in the light of Christ such as is found, for example, in the letter to the Hebrews. The Gentile seekers after Christ, on the other hand, needed to comprehend the meaning of Christ as the fulfillment of Jewish Messianic hopes (of which they were ignorant) as well as a moral code which their pagan Gentile backgrounds did not provide them. Their agenda had to do with two questions: What shall we believe? and How shall we conduct our lives?

The methodology of the Research Seminar on Christian Initiation (RSCI) involved bringing together a number of pastors from across Canada and the United States who had practical experience in initiating adults into the Christian faith in the context of their congregations for a week of work. The stated goals of the RSCI were as follows:

a)   to explore the theme of Christian initiation in the light of present congregational realities and practices;

b)   to examine the biblical, historical and theological roots of current practices;

c)   to design and experiment with a variety of approaches to Christian initiation with the goal of producing new instructional resources for the church.

Participants brought with them case studies of actual initiation events in their own ministries. The analysis of these case studies provided helpful information about the various kinds of situations with which they are working and for which resources need to be provided. Lectures on baptism in the early church and in Christian history (especially among the Anabaptists) were presented. In addition, the participants were introduced to curriculum development theory and gained actual experience in designing some resources to be field tested during the following year in their home settings.

During the second session of the RSCI in June 1993 reports from the field were given and evaluated. The participants then proceeded to refine further those procedures and materials which had proven to be helpful. An overall framework was designed within which the various steps in the initiation process proceed.

The Congregational Literature Division of the Mennonite Publishing House agreed to appoint writers and an editor to publish a handbook of Christian initiation. It was published under the title, *Welcoming Christians: A Guide to the Christian Initiation of Adults*. The writers are Jane Hoober Peifer and John Stahl-Wert; the editor is James E. Horsch.

One of the pastors who participated in the RSCI is Paul Versluis, pastor of the Foundation Mennonite Church in Erie, Pennsylvania. It was interesting to observe his vigorous probing and testing of the RCIA document and its theological presuppositions. He also contributed significantly to the designing of an initiation process based on Anabaptist/Mennonite theological assumptions and commitments.

Simultaneously, Paul was engaged in a Doctor of Ministry program at Pittsburgh Theological Seminary. The title of his doctoral paper is, *Making Disciples in the Congregation: A Guide to Christian Formation through the Process of Mentoring and the Experience of Congregational Worship*. Paul makes the point, in referring to the Roman Catholic document RCIA, that we should not be too proud to learn from others when they have useful insights. Accordingly, he "Anabaptised and Mennonitised" those elements in the RCIA which he found useful and made them his own.

Paul's doctoral project involved designing a series of Christian initiation services and carrying them out in the context of the Foundation Mennonite Church. Mentoring of companions is a key element in his approach. A series of services–the Service of Welcome, the Service of

Decision and the Service of Purity and Light--carry the process along and culminate in the Service of Baptism. Before outlining the order for each service, he describes the theology underlying the service. There is also an extended discussion of the theology and practice of mentoring as well as a description of nine Biblical images of mentoring.

The concluding chapter and appendix consist of evaluation forms which were used at the conclusion of this initial round as well as a report of the evaluation which was carried out.

This book is a case study of how the Christian initiation process was carried out in one Mennonite congregation and the learnings which were derived from it. It may be read alongside the official document which emerged from the RSCI and will hopefully be helpful to pastors and congregations who are looking for inspiration and assistance in guiding new believers into the way of Christ.

The Research Seminar on Christian Initiation was funded by a grant of $5000 from the Schowalter Foundation, Inc., and by contributions from the participants, their home congregations and their district conferences. The Commission on Education also provided some funds from their share of the Call to Kingdom Commitments fund.

Ross T. Bender, Director
Institute of Mennonite Studies
Elkhart, Indiana

CHAPTER I

THE CALL FOR MAKING DISCIPLES

The congregation at Foundation Mennonite Church believes that we are called by God to the ministry of "making disciples." The forty people in this congregation at Erie, Pennsylvania are willing to devote ourselves to this good work. This vision of making disciples has in view both the birth and the nurture of Christians, both a beginning and a beyond. We desire to call people who are not yet Christians to a new life with God and with God's people and to nurture them in this life. We, ourselves, desire to respond to God's call to go beyond and to "grow up in every way...in Christ" (Ephesians 4:15).

We have been called together for a purpose, "to make disciples" (Mt. 28:19). God worked for us and now we are being called to work with God. God's plan "to gather up all things in Christ" (Eph. 1:10) includes using us to do "good works" which we have been created in Christ Jesus to do (Eph.2:10). Although we do not have confidence in our own abilities to do this work, we are willing to depend upon God to complete the work God has begun among us.

We are willing to drink from other streams of spirituality, to listen to the best of other traditions. We want information and formation, we want to BE faithful and we do not mind DOING responsible things that may result in effective change. We are willing to work with Menno and rest with Martin and to eat with Merton.

The Need for Disciple Making

Within the congregation there is a threefold ministry, a three legged stool of worship, community, and mission. And, within the discipling process itself, there is a threefold responsibility, a three legged stool that stands as each holds its weight; Christ who sends the Holy Spirit, the congregation and the disciple.

Today the stool has tipped over. God is working, but the individual and congregational legs of the stool seem to have come unglued. The congregation is failing to make disciples. Our vision is fragmented, our resolve is indecisive, and our mind is confused. We do not know how to make disciples. We are so busy making everything else that we have little time left to give to this work. God is still working. People are coming to Jesus and maturing. But are we "making them like we used to"; are we making disciples that will last over the long haul? Today's Western disciple of Jesus tends to be undisciplined, immature, timid, a spiritual infant often conformed to culture. Do we want to work at our salvation? Are we adverse to suffering and discipline? Today's average congregation has abandoned its children. Disciples are orphaned, unwanted, home alone. The spiritual parents are absent, too busy to care. The church does not know how to parent her spiritual children. Children reflect their parents. We had no one to disciple us so we do not know how to disciple our children. This project is an attempt to find a way to take seriously Jesus' command "to make disciples." We desire to move from immaturity toward maturity in Christ, from fragmentation to wholeness, from information to formation of the mind, body, and heart. We desire to grow out of spiritual adolescence and become mature adults in Christ. Rather than blame God, the congregation, or the individual, we wish to admit the system's dysfunction and recognize our own responsibility. We desire to forgive the absence of spiritual mothers and fathers. Rather than try to find fault, we desire to accept, value, and thank those who have gone before us. We are willing to change and to do the best that we can to become obedient disciples of Jesus so that we can be spiritual mothers and fathers to our own children.

Responsibilities in Disciple Making

The responsibility of making disciples belongs to the local congregation, to God, and to the disciples themselves. These three strands of one rope must learn to work together.

1. The Role of the Congregation

The responsibility of the congregation in the process of making disciples is to equip and provide spiritual companions for those who seek to grow in Jesus Christ. The ideal would be that each Christian would have a spiritual companion or discipling group, that spiritual companions be equipped by the pastoral gifts within the congregation. The congregation disciples through the process of mentoring.

A second way in which the community participates in the process of making disciples is through worship. The worship experience is a primary context of discipleship. The congregation disciples people through mentoring and worship.

The congregation works to make disciples with the enabling power of the Holy Spirit. This is a joint effort. The congregation is yoked with the living Spirit of Jesus. Together with Jesus we pull the plow that prepares the people for the seed of God's word. Everything depends upon Jesus. The congregation must work in partnership with Christ to do the work of making disciples.

2. The Role of God

The congregation is the setting in which disciples are created and nurtured. God is present in this setting to make disciples just like the potter who forms the clay. With soiled hands, God molds and shapes the clay of our lives to become instruments fit for God's use, jars of clay that somehow hold the treasure of God's power (2 Corinthians 4:7). God is the stone mason who labors and sweats while carefully building a spiritual home. God joins us together as living stones by fitting us together upon the foundation of Christ. God is the builder whose purpose is to build a "dwelling in which God lives by His spirit" (Eph.2:22). God hammers us in the right place with the nail of Christ. In Christ, we are joined together. God is the gardener. With the farmer's love, God prunes the tree of the congregation and each season burns up the dead wood so that we may be as fruitful and alive as possible (John 15:1f). God is the artist, the potter, the mason, the builder, the farmer whose hard work makes disciples. We are the clay, the living stones, the branches. If the clay is not moist, if the stone is flawed and resists the perfecting touch of the mason, if the branch does not abide in Christ, we will not grow up. God makes all things good. If disciples are not being made, it must be because we are not doing our part.

3. The Role of the Disciple

Everything depends upon the disciples themselves. The disciple must respond to Christ and the congregation. As disciples, we must do our part. We must be faithful. It is God who is at work in the congregation enabling Christians to work together for the purpose of making disciples who in turn will be given the work of God in the world.

Whether or not disciples are made also depends upon those being discipled. Christ is the teacher, the congregation is the school, and the disciples are the students who must study and practice their lessons. Disciples are made as a result of commitment and obedience to the teachings of Christ.

Models for Discipling

1. Desired Characteristics of a Discipling Model

There is no one way to parent or to make disciples. But it seems prudent that a congregation chooses a model, seeks a common language, a mutual way of thinking, a shared practice, some common tools for the work of making disciples. The way we raise our disciples may not be the way another congregational family raises theirs, but we do need within the family a common language, some common expectations and disciplines.

Our congregation needs a model of discipling people toward the vision that we would "grow up in every way...into Christ" (Eph. 4:15). We want a model that emphasizes both the new birth and the mature life of the Christian community. We want a plan, a theology of the Christian life that is practical, simple, intentional, balanced, and rooted in the teaching and example of Jesus.

A model of discipling that is practical is one that is given to experience and practice. We do not want a model that merely informs the head, but one that forms the heart, the body, that forms Christ in us so that we actually live like Jesus. We want to be trained through practice so that we are equipped to do ministry, to work with and for Christ.

We want a model of discipling that is simple, designed for common folk. We do not want a discipling model for the religious elite, but a model designed to train the average, ordinary Christian to grow up in Christ. We are plain people who desire to put into practice a practical theology of the Christian life.

We desire a discipling model that is intentional, focused and purposeful. We want a model in which people are called to specific resolutions and commitments. We want a model that trains us through disciplines and hard work.

We want a balanced model of discipling, one that seeks to integrate worship, community, and mission. We do not want a plan that favors evangelism over social justice, the contemplative life over the holy life, the word over the Spirit, but we want a plan that seeks to make disciples desiring to grow in all these areas. A balanced model of discipling will not force us to choose between the individual and the community, but rather will affirm that we desire both mature saints and congregations.

A model of discipling that is rooted in the example and teaching of Jesus is a Christocentric one. We want to listen to the Gospels and as best we can derive our model from the example of Jesus. We desire to follow the way of Jesus and make disciples according to his pattern.

We also desire a model of discipling that acknowledges our own limitations, a humble model that is accepting of our weaknesses, that accepts and understands others who are at different stages of spiritual growth. We do not want a model that focuses on the proud and perfect, but one that is humble and human. The goal is maturity, but we must allow and accept our immaturity in a gracious manner.

2. The Congregational Discipling Model[1]

The Mennonite Board of Congregational Ministries is currently working on a vision and a model of congregational discipling. This vision provides a balanced way of thinking about making disciples that includes giving attention to community, worship, and mission. I have chosen to use the congregational vision and give it my own structural interpretation because I am biased toward inclusive, radical structures that favor new ways of thinking. In this model the whole system is engaged in the process of discipleship.

God is present in the congregation making disciples in at least three essential incarnational ways: through worship, community, and mission. God is present in congregational worship to make disciples by edification. God is present to form Christian character in the community of sisters and brothers. God is present in creating disciples in the mission of the congregation. A balanced diet of meaningful worship, loving community, and faithful service makes for healthy growing Christians.

In worship, we are shaped by God. Through prayer and praise, word and sacrament, the body of Christ is built by our personal and corporate relationship with God. God creates disciples through disciples being with Jesus (Mk. 3:14). In worship we are together with Christ.

In Christian community, we are transformed by the presence of Christ in sisters and brothers. Through mutual accountability, love, confession, forgiveness, spiritual friendships, mutual aid, and sharing wisdom, Christ is present to transform us into his likeness. This is a spirituality of participation rather than one of isolation.

In mission, it is our vocation to make known the presence of God through acts of service, peacemaking, doing good, and giving witness to God's truth through life-style and friendship evangelism. To grow in Christ each disciple is held accountable to the practice of doing good.

In each of the three areas, worship, community, and mission, we make disciples and we are made to be disciples. We both give and receive. We shape and are shaped by the presence of Christ as we go to God in worship, as we are gathered in love, and as we are scattered in mission into the world. People are discipled for participation in worship, community, and mission. We are also discipled by our participation in each area. In worship, we give to God and receive from God. In community, we give to one another and receive from one another. In mission, we serve and witness to another and we are served. We are given a sign of the presence of God alive and active in the world. As we witness to another, God can witness to us through this event. As we serve, we are served; as we disciple, we are discipled. We meet Christ in the friend, in the silence, and in the stranger. As we participate in the practice of worship, community, and mission, we can become aware of the grace of God equipping, empowering and enabling us to do the will of God, to be and to make disciples of Jesus.

3. The Rite of Christian Initiation of Adults as a Model

For our congregation to make disciples who grow in Christ through mutual participation in worship, community, and mission, we can utilize as a model an adaptation of the Rite of Christian Initiation of Adults developed by the Roman Catholic Church. Following Vatican II, the Roman Catholic Church prescribed a revision of their Rite of baptism for adults. This model of discipling views conversion as a process which divides the initiation experience into four sequential periods: 1. the period of Evangelization which is a time of inquiry, 2. the period of the Catechumenate which is a time of instruction, 3. the period of Enlightenment and Purification, a more intense preparation for Baptism and Membership, and 4. the period of Mystagogy which is a continuing time of nurture and participation in the life of the congregation.

Each period of initiation ends in a rite of passage that marks the transition from one period to the next. Following the period of Evangelization is the Rite of Acceptance into the order of catechumens. Following the period of the Catechumens is the Rite of Election marking the transition from instruction to spiritual preparation. Following the period of Purification and Enlightenment are the Rites that surround Baptism.

The RCIA is a practical model for discipling Christians, especially in relationship to worship. It represents an attempt to disciple the whole person, is intentional in its design to enable spiritual growth, and is a balanced approach that is given to worship, community, and mission. It is a Christocentric approach and its intention is to initiate persons into Christ and the Church.

The RCIA is a Catholic discipline for making disciples. In borrowing models we are laying down a proud spirit and admitting we can learn from others. There is no one pure Mennonite tool, no perfect Anabaptist vision for making disciples. The search for a pure discipleship is a form of ethnic pride. The fear of borrowing another's tools may be due to inordinate pride. The RCIA provides us with a new way of thinking about the process of making disciples.

4. The Role of Mentoring and Spiritual Friendships

I have referred to two conceptual models for making disciples: Congregational Discipling and the R.C.I.A. Both models encourage a mentor relationship, an intentional, spiritual friendship between a person being discipled and a mature Christian disciple from within the church community.

In the Catholic Order the mentor is called a sponsor. After the rite of Acceptance each person is given a sponsor. This mentoring relationship will continue for the duration of the initiation process which may last a year or more. In the Congregational Discipling model being advocated by the Mennonite Church, the mentor is a spiritual friend. One focus of this project will be on the mentor relationship in the initiation process: to be a mentor to persons who are coming for baptism and membership and to equip, encourage, and enable people to be spiritual mentors to others. I view the Congregational Discipling model as providing a cognitive framework for making disciples. The R.C.I.A. provides a practical embodied form in which to incarnate the idea of congregational discipling. The mentor relationship is the heart of this model of discipleship.

To be a spiritual friend is one way in which the congregation equips people for the work of the ministry. The mentor relationship is a primary way God works to develop spiritual health, authentic faith and maturity in the Christian community.

The mentor relationship is a pastoral relationship in which people serve as a guide who lead others to Jesus. The mentor relationship can provide a meaningful identity for pastors. Pastors are spiritually guided persons called by God to lead others to Christ through the power of the Holy Spirit. The Congregational Discipling model does not neglect the pastoral task, but defines the pastoral work in terms of spiritual friendships. The discipling process requires a personal relationship of spiritual intimacy. The felt need for many in the congregation is for this kind of holy relationship. The congregation disciples people by providing disciples with mentors/pastors.

Focus of Project

This project will be to develop an adapted form of the RCIA to serve our congregation. This will provide us a shared practice, a structural framework from which to go about making disciples. We will compose and participate in four worship services as a congregation: 1. A service of welcome, 2. A service of decision, 3. A service of dedication, and 4. A service of baptism. For each service I will provide a theological and biblical explanation of the meaning and purpose of the meeting.

A second focus of this project will be to equip and provide mentors for each person who is seeking to be discipled. There are eight people at this time who desire to be baptized. This project will be to equip and provide them with mentors. In addition to participating together in the four services, the mentors will be responsible to meet with their spiritual companion for one hour each week, before and after each service of worship. The goal is that both mentors and companions would through the process of spiritual friendships and shared worship grow up in all ways into Jesus Christ. I will provide materials and instruction to mentors on spiritual disciplines, mentoring, and a spiritual life interview derived from the gospel of Mark.

CHAPTER II

DISCIPLESHIP AS MENTORING

When I was just a lad, my uncle bought me a model airplane for Christmas. For days on end I tried to start the engine. I did everything I could but it was no use. The engine never started. Never mind the engine, I just pulled the plane around in circles, twirling it on its strings. Much later I learned that to start the engine I needed a battery. More than a battery I needed a model airplane buff, a mentor who could show me how to fly my machine. I loved that plane, and with a mentor it could have been even better.

I was thirteen. We were on our way to live in Alaska. While we were in Tacoma, Washington my mother and father took me to a store to buy a fishing pole. I did not know fishing, except in the farm creek. I told the salesperson that we were going "North to Alaska." He sold me a fine casting rod and reel. As I stood on the bank of a Canadian stream I gave that rod a mighty heave. The lure only went a few feet. No matter. I figured it needed some added weight so I tied on a lead sinker. We used them on the farm creek. The lure flew like a silver bird and sank like a rock. I caught my first snag and lost my first lure. I lost every lure that my father purchased. I felt like a fishing disaster. Later, while fishing off the spit in Homer Alaska I found out what was wrong. I owned a deep sea fishing rod and reel, a fine tool for the open sea but it was worthless on a small stream. What I needed was an angler to show me the difference between a casting and a spinning reel.

There are many kinds of mentors. Each trade, each discipline, has its own kind of mentor. If you desire to be a mason you become an apprentice to an experienced brick layer. You learn the trade by following the mentor's example.

In business it is often assumed that to get to the top a person needs a mentor. Those who have mentors will be more upwardly mobile, whereas those who do not will have a more difficult time. The younger employees hope that someone with power will choose to mentor them, befriend them, protect them, promote them.

In science, Robert Kanigel notes what he calls "The Mentor Chain."[2] If you are fortunate enough to be selected by a recognized scientist or lab, your chances of becoming a recognized, important scientist are far better than if you have no mentor connection. The younger scientist learns as an apprentice through the process of mentoring. The more experienced scientist parents the protégé, what Kanigel calls "passing on their genes."[3] Their way of thinking, their patterns, habits, ways of making meaning are handed down the mentor chain. Science is not a solitary affair but a family affair, a social affair in which scientists are trained as apprentices through the process of mentoring. Harriet Zuckerman studied 78 Nobel laureates and found that over half of them had worked for former Nobel laureates.[4] The scientific elite pass on their greatness, among other things. Jonathan Cole writes, "There are few scientists of note who did not have an identifiable sponsor."[5]

Robert Merton calls this the "Matthew Effect."[6] Those who have will be given more, whereas those who lack will have even what they have taken away. The scientific rich become richer while the scientific poor pass into obscurity. The same effect can be seen in other disciplines such as sports where Barry Bonds follows his father Bobby.

In education, the mentor serves as a guide. According to Larry Daloz mentors in the educational process do three distinct things: they support, challenge, and provide vision.[7] The feminine pole of support provides a safe holding environment, a secure protected home in which one is blessed and listened to. The masculine pole of challenge sets up special tasks and challenges for the student, creating a high standard of expectation. He writes, "Good teachers set high expectations for their students."[8] The mentor also provides the student vision. The student is taught to think like the mentor. The mentor provides the student with a model, a map, a tradition, a common language, a belief system. He says, "Like it or not, we will teach what we believe."[9] We can teach convictions and provide freedom for those we mentor to have another viewpoint. The mentor asks who we are and where are we going thereby enabling the student to mature. The students need a mentor to love and challenge them, to provide them with a model and vision.

The word mentor comes from Homer's Odyssey. Mentor is a trusted friend of Odysseus, appointed to care for Telemarkhos, Odysseus's son. Mentor appears to Telemarkhos in the form of the goddess of wisdom, Athene, daughter of the god Zeus. Mentor is to serve Telemarkhos in his search for reunion with his father. The impression is that without the help of the gods, without a mentor, Telemarkhos will not be reunited with his father.

Other famous mentors in literature are Gandolf in Tolkin's Lord of the Rings. There are the white-bearded Merlin of King Arthur's court, the 900 years old Yoda of Star Wars, the Skin Horse in the Velveteen Rabbit. These mentors arrive just at the right time to help the travelers along their path. Bruno Bettelheim says that the purpose of the mentor "is to remind us that we can, indeed, survive the terror of the coming journey and undergo the transformation by moving through, not around, our fear."[10]

Alcoholics Anonymous is an organization that recognizes the importance of a mentor in the process of recovery. They call the mentor a "sponsor" who is a person who helps another experience positive life change. Edward Sellner proposes that "A.A. and its understanding of the sponsor serve as a paradigm from which we can learn about sponsorship in the RCIA.[11] "Sponsors are not responsible for their companions' recovery, they are simply responsible to be friends who share their own story, giving witness to the power of grace in their own lives. A common story of grace emerges. Bill Wilson, co-founder of A.A., said that A.A. is "the story of how, under God's grace, an unsuspected strength has arisen out of great weakness."[12] If recovery is to continue it must be shared with a friend who acts as a living reminder that positive change is possible.

Gregory Michael Smith defines the role of the mentor in the process of the RCIA in the following ways: 1. the sponsor is an advocate of growth; 2. a listener of needs; 3. a prayer partner; 4. a reconciler of issues; and 5. a witness of the Christian life in action.[13]

Spiritual friends in the Bible are Mary and Elizabeth, Ruth and Naomi, Ananias and Barnabas who care for Paul. Ananias is used by God to bring Paul direction and healing. Barnabas mentors Paul (Acts 9:26). He befriends Paul, encourages, accepts and welcomes Paul when others would not. He defends Paul, he brings Paul to the Apostles, he listens to Paul and he shares Paul's story with the apostles. Paul in turn mentors Luke, Mark, Timothy, Silas, Euodia and Syntyche, Lydia, Titus, Onesimus, Priscilla, Aquila.

In conclusion, we make disciples through mentoring. Christians need mentors. Pastors and elders need mentors. It is unlikely that Christians will grow up into Jesus Christ without appropriate mentors. Mentoring is the primary and essential work of Christian leadership.

Jesus Calls People to the Work of Making Disciples

One day as Jesus walked beside the sea of Galilee, he saw Simeon and Andrew fishing. He called out to them, "Follow me and I will make you fish for people" (Mark 1:17). Immediately the brothers followed Jesus, leaving behind their nets, their boats, and their father.

The words of Jesus grabbed the brothers by their ears. He challenged them to leave their fishing nets behind and to learn from him how to fish for people, i.e., to bring people to God. With the assertive and authoritative snap of his word, Jesus landed his first two disciples. Jesus called Peter and Andrew to work for him. They would become his apprentices, he their mentor. Jesus would teach them the craft of spiritual formation, the art of making disciples.

On another occasion, a large crowd of people were coming to Jesus for healing and instruction. Jesus saw the people as confused and helpless, as spiritually hungry. His compassion awakened, he said to his disciples: "There is a big crop, but not many workers. So beg the harvest master to recruit workers for the harvest."[14] Jesus was once again

recruiting workers, calling upon God to send people to help him feed
those who are spiritually and physically hungry.

People coming to Jesus were told to work for food that endures
(John 6:27). We are not to work at laying up treasure on earth but to
work at laying up treasure in heaven (Mt.6:19-21). This is the work of
making disciples, the work of leading people to God. In offering the
disciples a job he was being honest and warning them that the pay is
minimum. Money cannot be a motive for discipleship.

Jesus took initiative. Speaking with authority he challenged
people to follow his way and to think like him. He did not wait for
people to choose him; he boldly chose them. Jesus was recruiting
soldiers for God's kingdom work. These disciples would be under his
command, they would pledge their allegiance to him. He would train
them, equip them, shape them into a unit to do the work of God. Jesus
would train them to fight like him. The church must be willing to
challenge people to conversion and Christian maturity by being bold
enough to encourage and provide mentoring relationships for all.
Susanne Johnson writes:

> ...there is no task more urgent than reorienting
> ministry in spirituality, especially through recovering
> the offices of teaching and spiritual direction in the
> Protestant church. This will require liberal mainline
> churches to overcome their natural shyness about the
> exercise of authority. We must become clear that it is
> possible to teach with real authority without becoming
> authoritarian.[15]

In this age of pluralism, the idea of intentionally seeking
disciples for Christ is often suspect. Some insist that the true spiritual
director would never wander around looking for someone to direct.[16]
But we can be as bold and aggressive as Jesus. Some are seeking for
spiritual mothers and fathers to be their mentors in faith.

From the beginning, God is portrayed as a God who works.
"On the seventh day God finished the work He had done" (Gen. 2:2).
Although God rested from the work of creation, God did not retire.
Jesus would argue, "My father is still working, and I am also working"
(John 5:17). Jesus was hungry to complete the work that God had given
him to do (John 4:34). John the Baptist summarizes the work of Christ
as follows: Jesus is the "Lamb of God who takes away the sin of the
world" (John 1:29) and he is the one "who baptizes with the Holy Spirit"
(John 1:33). Jesus has accomplished his work of setting us free from the
powers of evil, sin and death. He saves us from the powers of evil; he
saves us for the kingdom of God. He sends us the Holy Spirit (John
14:26). Although reason cannot adequately comprehend this work of

Christ, as Christians we believe that his work of salvation is sufficient and effective.

Jesus finished the work God had given him to do, yet there is more work to be done. Jesus said, "And I, when I am lifted up from the earth, will draw all people to myself" (John 12:32). Jesus was lifted up on the cross, he died, and he is risen. Christ now works as a spiritual magnet through whom God draws all people and all things home to God. Paul writes that God has a plan for the fullness of time: "To gather up all things in [Christ]" (Eph. 1:10), a vision to unite all things in Christ (Col. 1:20, Rom. 8:21). This plan turns on the hinge of the victory of Christ risen from the dead. Paul calls this plan of God a mystery that we cannot now fully understand, the details of which are unclear (1 Cor. 13:12). We can be confident that God who began this work will bring it to completion (Phil. 1:6).

God's plan included work for the church. God has set us free from the powers of evil and made us alive in Christ. This work of Christ is God's gift to us. Now that we are alive and free we are called to use our lives and freedom to serve God. Paul writes, "For we are what [God] has made us, created in Christ Jesus for good works, which God prepared beforehand to be our way of life" (Eph. 2:10). In meeting Jesus we are presented with a choice: to work for ourselves, or to leave our nets and to work with God to bring about a new creation. We do not need to work for our salvation but we are invited to work with the God of our salvation. We work for God, we work with God, and we work together with our sisters and brothers in the church to continue the work of Christ, the work of making disciples.

There is work to be done. God makes real demands upon us. Our participation together with God in the work of making disciples is essential, important, necessary. God does not make disciples alone. We become God's "utensils" (2 Tim. 2:21), "instruments" (Acts 9:15), "clay jars" (2 Cor. 4:7), the tools God uses to shape Christ into the character of others. Of course, we cannot make disciples by ourselves (John 15:5). Our competency for this ministry comes from God (2 Cor. 3:5,6). As God's servants, our task is not to make disciples by ourselves, but to participate in the work God is doing in their lives. We are like the donkey that carried Jesus into Jerusalem. We carry Christ to the people. Because we are yoked to Christ, this work will not prove to be impossible (Mt. 11:28f). Like John the Baptist, we know we are not the Messiah, but the Lord may use us as mentors to prepare the way of God in the life of our companion. To mentor is to be a priest.

The Priority of Discipleship and the Ministry of Mentoring

In Matthew 28:16-20 Jesus clarifies the primary agenda of the church to be the task of making disciples. "Making disciples" is the

central focus of this passage, the first work of the church. We make
disciples by "baptizing them in the name of the Father, and of the Son
and of the Holy Spirit, and teaching them to obey everything that I have
commanded you" (Mt. 28:19-20). The goal is obedience to Christ. This
agenda for the church given by Christ begins with the empowerment of
Christ's authority and ends with Christ's promise to be with us. His
authority and presence with us enables us to participate in the work of
making disciples. Just as Ford makes cars and trucks, the church is in
the business of making disciples.

For Anabaptists, discipleship has been a priority. This focus is
seen in the current Model of Congregational Discipling in which
discipleship is the heart of the vision. This viewpoint is shared by
Stanley Hauerwas and William Willimon who write, "... the main
political task of the church is the formation of people who see clearly the
cost of discipleship and are willing to pay the price."[17]

Perhaps Jesus was thinking about the disciples' tendency to
argue about who or what is the greatest. His last words establish a
priority. Not evangelism, worship, the Word, the Sacraments, prayer,
justice or peace, but discipleship. The practical, hard, ordinary work of
making disciples comes first. Discipling is the center we seek.

Different Christian traditions tend to emphasize a particular
point of view, often setting up a competitive spirit over who or what is
the greatest. One ideal picture of the church describes the church as a
family.

> They devoted themselves to the apostles' teaching and
> fellowship, to the breaking of bread and the prayers.
> Awe came upon everyone, because many wonders
> and signs were being done by the apostles. All who
> believed were together and had all things in common:
> they would sell their possessions and goods and
> distribute the proceeds to all, as any had need. Day
> by day, as they spent much time together in the
> temple, they broke bread at home and ate their food
> with glad and generous hearts, praising God and
> having the goodwill of all the people. And day by
> day the Lord added to their number those who were
> being saved. (Acts 2:42-47)

In this passage we imagine evangelicals as majoring in a
devotion to the "apostles' teaching", with an emphasis on a devotion to
the Word. Those inclined toward Christian community are committed
to "fellowship." A liturgical or sacramental viewpoint will focus
attention on "the breaking of bread" as communion, whereas a non-
liturgical lens will see "breaking of bread" as the simple hospitality of a
shared meal. Those who are contemplative major in "prayer," while the

charismatics anticipate "signs and wonders," hoping to experience "awe come upon everyone." Christians who advocate peace and justice will emphasize "all things in common," interpreting it to mean simplicity, downward mobility, a fair and equal distribution of goods. Praise and worship enthusiasts will want to spend a good amount of their time "together in the temple" praising God with generous and single minded devotion, while the evangelists count each day the number of converts "being saved."

A shared common life, a balanced spirituality will be more likely to occur if discipleship is seen as the central work of the church. A competitive spirit may be less likely if we actually make disciples, where every Christian is discipled and every Christian has the opportunity to join in this common work of making disciples. These different streams of spirituality need to live together as family with each contributing to the common good. The Christian community is a spiritual parent to each disciple, nurturing everyone toward the goal of maturity in Christ.

The Goal of Discipleship as Christian Maturity

The goal of discipleship is that we would in all ways grow up into Jesus Christ, that we would become mature. Paul defines maturity as "the measure of the full stature of Christ" (Eph. 4:13). Jesus's command to "be perfect" is best translated as "be mature."[18] This maturity is usually understood as the process of sanctification. Susanne Johnson says, "Sanctification refers to the actual formation of Christian character."[19] Sanctification is an event and a process in which our character is changed and shaped by the energy of God's grace. This conversion and transfor- mation of life is normatively a lifelong process that occurs within the holding environment of the church.

A mature Christian is one who has learned to obey Jesus. The goal of discipleship is to teach disciples to obey Jesus (Mt. 28:20). This is an obedience that is to some extent habitual, an obedience of practice, where the disciple becomes willing to do the will of God. David Watson agrees that "the mark of a mature Christian... was a consistent obedience to God."[20] In some contexts one may prefer to use the word faithfulness rather than obedience. The mark of a mature Christian is that they are faithful to Christ.

Obedience to Christ is the fruit of our relationship with him. As Bonhoeffer says, "Obedience to the call of Jesus never lies within our own power."[21] The obedience of the disciple is seen as the result of the effect of Christ upon them. They were not taught to depend upon their own strength but to depend upon Jesus. We are faithful because of the grace of God, because of the faithfulness of Christ.

The essential Christian character, the essential obedience of the Christian life, is to love as Jesus loved (John 15:12). Ray Anderson says, "Love is the most valued evidence of spiritual maturity in the New Testament."[22]

The mature Christian is a holy person. Holiness is defined by Alan Kreider as "a living force, unseen but very real."[23] Holiness is the very presence of God, the essential nature of the sacred.[24] We are made holy, transformed into the image of Christ, by the energy and power of God. James Fenhagen writes, "Holiness is the fruit of our association with Jesus."[25]

Holiness does not mean perfection, or wholeness. One can be healthy and whole but not holy. Ray Anderson says, "While wholeness is not a presupposition of holiness... holiness anticipates and seeks wholeness"[26] Holiness is not a natural, evolutionary, human capacity but the different, alien power of God's life active within us. Christian maturity defined as obedience, love and holiness, is an obedience, a love and a holiness that is beyond our ability to develop. Our lives are transformed by the Holy Spirit. Scott Peck's insight that we have within us an upward thrust toward wholeness, health and holiness must not be understood as a natural evolutionary tendency but as the result of the Holy Spirit active in our lives.[27] Spiritual growth is not necessarily sequential or occurring in stages that can be mapped. Rather, spiritual growth occurs in transformational moments created by an encounter with God.

Thomas Merton says, "A holy person is one who is sanctified by the presence of the action of God in him."[28] God's grace is "God's very presence and action within us."[29] He calls the Holy Spirit the "sweet guest dwelling in our soul."[30]

Obedience, love and holiness are the fruits of God's grace. God's grace transforms us, but we can complicate this by denying that we have nothing to do. God has a part and so do we. We must abide in Jesus.

Dallas Willard calls holiness "something else."[31] Holiness is the reality of Jesus Christ. Jesus defines what holiness, obedience and love are. Robert Fabing writes, "What Jesus does is what holiness is. What Jesus says is what holiness is. What Jesus experienced is what holiness is, because Jesus is holiness."[32]

Christian maturity is social as well as personal holiness. John Wesley once wrote, "The gospel of Christ knows of no religion, but social; no holiness but social holiness."[33] God is at work in the world to bring about obedience, love, and holiness. There is no holiness without justice. Spiritual disciplines, worship, spiritual friendship, prayer, scripture, community, sacraments are intended to prepare us for mission. They teach us how to depend upon God, then to serve God in the world.

Holiness is about vision, a vision of God. We learn to see God in all things. We begin to see the world through the eyes of Christ. The spiritual life is not intended to shut our eyes to the world, but to open them to see the world from God's perspective.

To be obedient and holy, we must live in relationship with Christ.   Kenneth Davis writes, "Anabaptist theology may be best expressed as a theology of holiness."[34] An Anabaptist perspective on holiness affirms a "limited divinization," where God's grace transforms character. This includes an intentional pursuit of holiness, discipleship in life and renunciation of the world.   He concludes, "The ascetic principle, namely the pursuit of holiness, is a fundamental principle in Anabaptist theology."[35] The goal of discipleship is a holy life.

The Mentor as an Example of Christ

The mentor provides an example, a model to follow.   The Christian mentor represents a practical living example of the presence of Jesus.   Every mentor is a priest, every sponsor a pastor to one's companion. As Paul says, "...we have this treasure in clay jars, so that it may be made clear that this extraordinary power belongs to God and does not come from us" (2 Cor. 4:7) Christ lives in us and we become his example, his vessel, his instrument of grace to build up our companion toward maturity, "to the measure of the full stature of Christ" (Eph. 4:13).

Jesus modeled what he taught. His teaching informed the mind while his life provided a living model of his teaching. He taught with the authority of a living example. His teaching challenged and set an objective standard—"Love your enemies"—while his example showed how it could be done. One picture is worth a thousand words. We need more than Bible instruction. We need to see the Word of God embodied in people. We need the epistles and the apostles.

In our video generation we have an abundance of information but a scarcity of models. Pastors are too busy to be mentors. Our spiritual parents have left us home alone with a Christian VCR and a book. To change this we need to call Christians to the task of spiritual formation where each Christian is mentored.

For Anabaptist's, Jesus is not just an object of worship, a moral teacher, a Savior. Jesus is also a model, an example to follow in life. Walter Klaassen writes,

> A major feature of Anabaptist Christology was the weight placed on the function of Jesus as model and example. That involved an emphasis on his human life with his actions and words as described in the gospels.[36]

There is a strong tendency in Anabaptist spirituality that draws us to follow Jesus, to imitate Christ.[37]

We imitate Christ by imitating other Christians. Mentoring is a way to practice the imitation of Christ. We are a practical people. We want to see it done. When something matters we say, "Don't just tell me, show me." Show me how you pray, how you forgive and confess your sins. We are family and we grow up into Christ by following examples. Mentoring as modeling is indispensable to maturing in the Christian life.

Jesus told his disciples to follow his example. He wanted them to be willing to serve and to be served by one another, so he taught humility by washing their feet. Jesus showed them the meaning of humble service. He did not merely define humility but acted the part so that they could see it embodied. He said, "I have set you an example, that you also should do as I have done to you" (John 13:15).

Paul urged the Corinthians: "Be imitators of me, as I am of Christ" (1 Cor. 11:1). He conveyed to them that he had become their spiritual parent and appealed to them to "be imitators of me" (1 Cor. 4:10). He insisted that Timothy "set the believers an example in speech and conduct, in love, in faith, in purity" (1 Tim. 4:12). He urged Timothy to "put these things into practice, devote yourself to them, so that all may see your progress" (1 Tim. 4:15). As models we are to practice our faith so that our practice becomes an example to our companions. We are not responsible for the faith of our companions but we are responsible to be faithful ourselves to Christ. Our own obedience is enough. And if we disobey and prove again that we are human, then we can be an example to our companion of repentance.

The scriptures indicate various kinds of behavior mentors may model. The companion may consider the outcome of their mentor's way of life and "imitate their faith" (Heb. 7:7). We need to be with people who have faith in Christ and who have the faith of Christ. Mentors model forgiveness, love, and sacrifice (Eph. 4:32,5:2). Mentors are models of yieldedness and humility.

Paul writes, "Brothers and sisters, join in imitating me, and observe those who live according to the example you have in us" (Phil. 3:17). The example they saw modeled in Paul was a willingness to suffer and bear the cross. Paul says, "Follow my example as I follow the example of Christ" (I Cor. 11:1). The example he is referring to is that "Christ did not please himself" (Rom. 15:3), he was "obedient to the point of death" (Phil. 2:8).

Peter writes, "For to this you have been called, because Christ also suffered for you, leaving you an example, so that you should follow in his steps" (1 Pet. 2:21). We need examples, not just stories of people who are trying not to fight with their fists or their words. We need examples of people who are trying to bless those who curse them. We need examples of people who make peace through the power of the resurrection of Christ. Living in America with its religion of self we need examples of people who sacrifice, who do not live to please themselves, who surrender their self in trust to God.

Mentors model hard work. Paul writes to Titus, "Show yourself in all respects a model of good works" (Tit. 2:7). Some of the people were freeloading. While Paul was with them he worked to earn his keep. He worked hard "as an example to imitate" (2 Thess. 3:9). When I worked with Jack as a laborer in building house foundations, the example of my leader's hard work was a model for me to follow.

The mentor models leadership. Peter says, "Do not lord it over those in your charge, but be examples to the flock" (1 Pet. 5:3). To grow up on Christ we need leaders who lead us to God and not to themselves. What a motive for holiness! We persevere and labor for our "children in the Lord." We are willing to be disciplined by God because we have a responsibility to be an example. It is the same motive that is effective in A.A.. We stay sober because we are sponsors. We do the best we can because someone is following us. We don't hit the jerk in the mouth because the children are watching. Sometimes that's the best we can do. We grow in Christ because someone is depending on us. Our obedience is not perfect, but our best is good enough.

Biblical Images of Mentoring

1. The Mentor as a Stretcher Bearer
   Then some people came, bringing to (Jesus) a paralyzed man, carried by four of them (Mark 2:3).

Jesus was returning to his own city, Capernaum. Previously, he had healed the sick in the area. Jesus left town early in the morning even though many people were searching for him. Perhaps this paralyzed man was one of those who were searching for Jesus, only to find that he was gone. Now that Jesus had returned he was not about to miss him a second time. He wanted to be healed. He came to Jesus out of his need. Because of his disability he had to be carried. There was a crowd around Jesus. They decided to make a hole in the roof and lower their friend to Jesus through the hole. The stretcher bearers brought the man and his need to Jesus. Jesus saw the faith of those who carried the paralytic, he forgave the man his sins and he healed him.

The mentor is a stretcher bearer, one who faithfully carries another into the presence of Christ, believing in the power of Christ to forgive and heal those we bring to him. Spiritual friendship is a ministry of referral. Our responsibility is not to heal but to witness and participate in the healing and forgiveness of Christ. The sponsor refers and guides another to Jesus.

James Fowler writes, "The sponsor is one who walks with you, one who knows the path and can provide guidance. The sponsor is one who engenders trust and proves trustworthy in supporting you in difficult passages or turns."[38]   Christian sponsors guide their companions to God.

Doctors focus on disease, counselors on problems, lawyers attend to injustice, while Christian mentors focus on God. The mentor specifically leads people to God. In other professions what happens depends upon the skill, ability, and educational expertise of the professional. "I can do it," says the dentist, and who would go to a dentist who would not say "I can do it"?

In making disciples we are operating in a different dimension where ego strength, skills, expertise are not the critical factors. The sponsor says, "I cannot do it, I do not know how, but I will refer you to God. Sponsors are operating in the realm of grace. I am not in control. The best I can do is be a relaxed presence and direct my companion with my weak arms into the strong arm of God.

The sponsor is not a counselor or therapist. It is not our responsibility to solve or fix another's problems. We do not even need to help people but we call people to the God who helps. We do not help people to adjust but we call people into a relationship with God. Unless asked, the sponsor does not even need to give advice. God is always the spiritual director, we are always stretcher bearers. God is the one who will "guide us on the right path" (Psalm 23:3). The sponsor can let go of the impossible task of playing God and take up the enjoyable task of referring people to Christ. We do our best as sponsors when we do no harm, do not get in the way of what God is already up to in our friend's life. Sponsors do not want their companions to depend upon them, but upon God. We may give our companion a hard or soft word, a scripture, a prayer, even rebuke or correction and then we leave them with God. The sponsor may be a catalyst to spiritual growth but not the cause.

2. The Mentor as a Sheep Dog

> For you were going astray like sheep, but you have returned to
> the shepherd and guardian of your souls   (1 Peter 2:25).

The mentor is not the shepherd but a sheep dog who turns the companion toward Jesus the "Good Shepherd." Acting as an "example to the flock" (1 Peter 5:3), we do not lord it over the sheep by turning their attention to ourselves, to our abilities. We are not proud but humble enough to realize that there is very little we can do in our own strength to guard or correct our friends. They must be free to fail, fall, or stray. Sofield and Juliano write that we need to "help people move from a spirituality of perfection to a spirituality of failure."[39] Thomas Finger says that "true spirituality involves humbly acknowledging one's limitations."[40] Without the good shepherd we are all lost. The best we can do for our companions is to turn them toward the good shepherd, guide them home to Jesus.

3. The Mentor as a Lens

> Let us run with perseverance the race that is set before us, looking to Jesus the pioneer and perfecter of our faith (Hebrews 12:1-2).

Mentors turn their companions' attention to God, guiding them to fix their eyes on Jesus who is the author and perfecter of their faith. As the young driver is told to keep both eyes on the road, the companion is told to look to Jesus. The mentor is blind and cannot see. Only God can see. Kenneth Leech says, "At heart, the contemp- lative is one who sees clearly, sees with the eyes of God."[41] Hans Urs von Balthasar writes, "Christian faith is a participation in Christ's vision"[42]
One autumn afternoon I was helping friends move their belongings. The "white rabbit," a dear old truck, was packed full of stuff. At dusk, I drove the "rabbit" the thirty miles to town. As I arrived my friends burst out of their car waving their arms, exclaiming, "Have you ever seen such a magnificent sunset?" Regretfully, I had been thinking about other things. I did not even notice the sun go down. Mentors remind their companions to look into the light of Christ, to see themselves and the world from God's perspective.

> If I go forward, he is not there; or backward, I cannot perceive him; on the left he hides, and I cannot behold him; I turn to the right, but I cannot see him. But he knows the way that I take; when he has tested me, I shall come out like gold (Job 23:8-10).

We may not often be able to perceive God, yet we may come to trust that God knows our way, that God sees us as gold.

4. The Mentor as a Hearing Aid.

> "Spiritual direction is listening."[43]

The apprentice must listen to the instruction of the master. It did not matter that the disciples were ordinary and uneducated folk (Acts 4:13). What mattered was that they would listen to Jesus. Jesus said, "Pay attention to how you listen; for to those who have, more will be given; and to those who do not have, even what they seem to have will be taken away" (Luke 8:18). Those who listen to Jesus will be given more. The good soil in the Parable of the Sower are people who hear and hold fast to the word Jesus speaks (Luke 8:15). Obedience begins with hearing Jesus.

Mentors are ones who listen to God and to one's companion. My beloved children often want my attention, they want me to listen to them. This is a sacrifice where I must let go of self and give them attention. Mentors listen to their companions' stories, their fears, their dreams, their body language, their response to scripture. A mentor does not have to say very much, if anything at all. We do not need to speak the perfect word or say something profound. We just need to give our attention to the Lord and our friend. We need to listen but we do not need to speak. To be given attention is a marvelous experience. "Listening is waiting upon God in watchful expectancy."[44] We need to learn to listen patiently for God, to be expectant and attentive to the Lord's coming.

In commenting on the story Jesus told about the Son of Man coming at an unexpected hour (Luke 12:40), Basil Pennington writes, "We ought to be always awaiting his coming. I do not think this necessarily refers to the last coming...but the daily visits of grace and Presence, many of which we probably miss because we are not attentive, do not hear the knock."[45] Mentors encourage their companions to listen. This is why it is important for us to have times of quiet, solitude and Sabbath rest. We need to learn to know and hear the voice of Jesus (John 10:27).

Eli was a mentor to Samuel. He helped Samuel discern the voice of God. He directed Samuel to God, told him to go lie down, be quiet, and listen for the word of God. Spiritual mentors direct their companions to rest, to go lie down, be quiet and listen for God. They direct us to say, "Speak, Lord, for your servant is listening" (1 Samuel 3:9).

Mentoring is listening and sharing stories. Jesus told the disciples stories. For the first few meetings perhaps all the mentor may choose to do is to listen to stories. When the time is right we may share our own stories with our companion. Our lives are an unfinished book God may use to witness to God's grace. Our own stories, especially when they show how grace arises out of our own weakness, can be a powerful witness to the grace of God. Frederick Breuchner points out that "at its heart most theology, like most fiction, is essentially autobiography."[46]

5. The Mentor as a Friend

You are my friends if you do what I command you. I do not call you servants any longer, because the servant does not know what the master is doing; but I have called you friends, because I have made known to you everything that I have heard from my Father (John 15:14,15).

Spiritual formation, the development of Christian character, sanctification, requires face to face relationships. We need people, not just books. Spiritual growth requires friendship. The key to spiritual growth is love. Love is the primary spiritual discipline, the first need, the best part of spiritual growth. A mentor is a personal friend, one who loves his/her companion. C. S. Lewis once said that "all friends are a gift from God."[47] The love of Christ defines the heart of the mentor relationship. It is love that heals, love that brings forth growth and maturity. We obey Christ when we love our companion. Human love directs our attention to God. We make disciples by loving them. The mentor is a friend, an angel sent from God to help us to grow in Christ. The best mentors in the church will always be those who love. Merton writes,

> ...the Holy Ghost was waiting to show me the light, in his own light. And one of the chief means he used, and through which he operated, was human friendship....All our salvation begins on the level of common and natural and ordinary things...[48]

There are no perfect sponsors but the best sponsors are those who love through the ministry of friendship. This "Soul Friend" is caring, patient, honest and truthful, has nothing to hide, and is open to sharing his/her own story. Spiritual friends are compassionate, willing to suffer with another in their pain. They are civil, have a basic respect for another's values and beliefs, are open to questions, hospitable, and full of hope. They are not arrogant, proud, boastful, but humble. They believe (1 Cor. 13:4-7). This kind of love will endure. This is the kind of stuff from which disciples are made.

To love means that we will make ourselves available to our companions. We will spend time with them. Mark writes that Jesus appointed the disciples "to be with him" (Mark 3:14). There were told that apart from him they could do nothing (John 15:5). They needed to abide with Jesus. There is no discipleship without intimacy with Jesus, without a commitment to a personal relationship with Jesus Christ. Only by being with Jesus would they learn to trust him, understand him, recognize his purpose, his love. Only through intimacy with Jesus would they be given the grace to obey him, to suffer as he suffered, to love as he loved.

Mentors may be very holy persons, wise and loving, but if they are not available then they are worthless as mentors. Discipling takes time and if people are too busy they should not choose or be chosen to be a mentor.

6. The Mentor as a Person of Prayer

"Epaphras...is always wrestling in prayer for you..." (Col. 4:12)

As mentors we pray for our companion, and we pray with our companion. We learn to pray, as does our companion, by praying. A fine example of this is Jesus as he prays for his disciples, his own spiritual companions, in John 17.

Jesus had "finished the work" (v.4) that God had given him to do. This work involved revealing God to others. Jesus said, "I made your name known to those who you gave me from the world." (v.3,6,25) This work included giving to the disciples the word of God; "for the words that you gave to me I have given to them." (v.8,14) This work included the task of praying for the disciples (v.9), that God would protect them (v.11, 15), and that they would be filled with the joy of Christ (v.13). He prayed for his companions whom he sent into the world that "they may know that you have sent me and have loved them even as you have loved me" (v.23). This work included living a holy life for the disciple's sake. "And for their sakes I sanctify myself, so that they also may be sanctified in truth" (v.19).

This example shows us that the sponsors' work is to reveal God to their spiritual companions, to make Jesus known. Sponsors seek to give to their companions the word of God. Sponsors pray for their companions: that God would protect them, that they would be one, that they would be made holy by the word and truth, that they would be filled with the Holy Spirit and the joy of Christ. Sponsors pray that God would send their companions into the world, that their companions would reveal to the world the love and truth of God. Sponsors seek to live a holy life for the sake of those they are caring for.

Five of us once committed ourselves to pray daily for each other. Despite our best intentions, none of us were able consistently to keep the discipline. Because I have found the discipline of prayer difficult I have borrowed forms of prayer from others. One prayer discipline that I have found helpful is to pray the scripture.

As I read scripture I notice a passage or phrase that seems appropriate for me to pray for my companion. I compose a prayer from the passage. For example, "God, turn the heart of my friend to his children, and turn the hearts of his children to him" (Mal 4:6).

Another way to pray for your companion is to read scripture and focus on a word or phrase. I allow my attention to dwell on this word. I write it down, I think about the idea with my mind, envision the word with my imagination, experience the word in my heart. I allow the word to occupy my mind and descend into my heart. I turn the phrase into a prayer and repeat the prayer during my day. I attempt to receive the word, believe the word, and I am willing to share this "living and active Word." This kind of prayer is called the "Prayer of the Heart," or "Lectio Divina." If the Word of God just dwells in our heads and does not descend into our hearts we get a headache. If the Word just lies in our hearts it will cause heartburn. The Word of God should move from our heads to our hearts, to our hands in which we share it

with another. We pass it on. The strength of spiritual friends is found
in their prayers.

7. The Mentor as a Channel of Blessing
> Truly I tell you, whoever does not receive the kingdom of God
> as a little child will never enter it. And [Jesus] took [the
> children] up in his arms, laid his hands on them, and blessed
> them (Mk. 10:15,16).

The spiritual mother/father conveys God's blessing to these
"children of God." The sponsors may touch their companions or kneel
and bless them in the name of Christ. The first thing God did after
creating Adam and Eve was to bless them (Gen. 1:28). The first word
Jesus heard after his baptism was a word of blessing; "This is my son,
the beloved, with whom I am well pleased" (Mt. 3;17). A mentor is
God's priest through whom God sends holy rain into the life of one's
companion. At first the younger is blessed by the elder, "the inferior is
blessed by the superior" (Heb. 7:7). The second movement is when
those who are blessed flourish and themselves become a channel of
blessing through whom the water of God flows into the desert. The
mentor is twice blessed, by God and by one's companion.

For some companions the blessing of the parent is absent,
unexpressed, confusing, or conditional. Some will have experienced
more cursing than blessing, perhaps rarely having experienced the joy
of being blessed. The blessing of God brings hope. God's blessing is
medicine, an antidote for apathy and depression. When we are blessed
by God it is as if God is laughing, smiling upon us.

To bless is to affirm. The sponsor is one who smiles, laughs.
We give thanks for our spiritual companions. We could even anoint
their head with the oil of joy. We might share with them a quality we
find in them that we would like to emulate, something we admire in
them. They are special.

Laying our hands upon their shoulder, we might pray over
them the words of Numbers 6:24-26, or Romans 15:13. Touching them
gently, smiling, we might say, "May the joy of Jesus be in you, and may
your joy be complete" (John 15:11).

The more difficult their suffering, the more important it is to
bless them. To bear the cross of Christ we need often to receive the joy
of Christ. The sponsors and their companions could set aside ten
minutes a day for a week to give thanks for as many things as they can
think of, to think about what is good. Perhaps for awhile we could both
try to keep a discipline of "blessing those who curse us."

People hunger for God's blessing. We want to delight in God,
to take pleasure in God. The mentor relationship is one means of
experiencing God's blessing. Often the blessing is simply scripture that

we memorize. We have been given the authority to forgive sins, which is a fine blessing.

8. Spiritual Community

Obey your leaders and submit to them, for they are keeping watch over your souls and will give an account. Let them do this with joy and not with sighing - for that would be harmful to you (Heb. 13:17).

We cannot go far in the Christian life alone. The isolated Christian lacks the giftedness of others to mature. A primary task for sponsors is to hold their companions accountable for discipleship. Sponsors are Christian leaders who with joy keep watch over their companions' souls, holding them accountable to spiritual disciplines.

Spiritual community is for people who recognize their spiritual poverty, who know they are powerless to grow in Christ alone. They admit they cannot in their own strength form their own Christian character. They know they are imperfect but they will not allow their own imperfections nor the imperfections of others to keep them from drawing near to God who alone is able to make us whole.

Spiritual care provides an opportunity to encourage the practice of confession. We do not require confession but neither should we avoid it. When confession is appropriate one may confess to God, to us, to one they have wronged, or to someone else. The sponsor asks, "Have you confessed your sins?" The sponsor may speak a word of forgiveness. We can heed Bonhoeffer's advice that "...only those who make confession should hear confession."[49] What is shared and confessed is confidential.

Mentors hold their companions accountable to the practice of spiritual disciplines. Spiritual community is for those who are willing to work at their salvation with the energy God provides (Phil. 2:12). Christian formation is not automatic, there are no short cuts, no universal map that works for everyone. As Oswald Chambers once said, "The practice is ours, not God's."[50]

To go to God alone is the easy way. If we really want to grow up in Christ we will have to practice disciplines of the Christian life. Practice makes perfect. We must be accountable. Jesus said that there are two ways, a wide gate with an easy road or a narrow gate with a hard road (Mt. 7:13). The hard road with the narrow gate is the way of spiritual community, accountability, and discipline.

Spiritual disciplines are defined by Dallas Willard as "...activities of mind and body purposefully undertaken, to bring our personality and total being into effective cooperation with the divine order."[51] These disciplines enable us to yield to the grace of God. God is at work changing the old habits of the flesh by replacing them with new habits of the Spirit. The discipline is ours whether we are learning baseball or learning to love an enemy. Maturity is not developed without labor and practice.

We do not need to find the perfect discipline. What is important is that we practice some form of spiritual discipline. Prayer, scripture, worship, community, confession, celebration are some of the disciplines we have been speaking about to this point. Blue collar spirituality is not fancy. Bonhoeffer writes, "Spiritual care is quite modest."[52] In spiritual friendship we are usually concerned with the ordinary stuff of our daily lives. Going to bed and getting up on time, parenting, unemployment, overeating, sexuality, making decisions, exercise, habits, being too busy. We are formulating a domestic piety. Spiritual friendship is designed to focus on our experience of God in ordinary life. The idea is to remain faithful, to keep at it, whether we have flashy experiences or not.

People are so consumed by their own pain and confusion that they have little energy left to devote to caring for others. Hopefully, spiritual community will work at least to turn the sponsor toward the pain of others in the world.

We must not ignore the practice of correction or rebuke. There are teachable moments in life and when God provides one we must not let the opportunity pass because of our own fear of authority. If God provides an opportunity for corrective discipline, we can be willing to gently follow God' leading. How many children and disciples never grow up because of a lack of wise parental discipline.

9. The Mentor Encourages Good Deeds
> And let us consider how to provoke one another to love and good deeds (Hebrews 10:24).

The mentor is to be a model of "good works," being involved in Christian service. Jesus went about "doing good" (Acts 10:38). Paul urges Titus, "Show yourself in all respects a model of good work" (Titus 2:6). The mentor models good works as a productive and practical example of Christ's love (Titus 3:14). Doing good is one way we are useful to God (2 Tim. 2:20), a way in which we give glory and witness to God (Mt. 5.16). Doing good is a spiritual discipline for all Christians (Col. 1:10).

Doing good is a practical way to respond in love to violence and evil, a way we learn through experience and faith in Christ to "overcome evil with good" (Rom. 12:9,21). Service to others is a means and an end to spiritual growth.[53] It is what we do when we consider how much suffering exists and how insignificant are our efforts. In answer to the question, "What can I do?", we do something, anything that is good. We put our own house in order, we serve another regardless of how insignificant it may seem.

Mentors hold their companions accountable to this discipline of "love and good deeds," provoking them to serve others (Heb. 10:24). The mentor may serve a proud companion by setting an example of one who will also receive. Those who are by nature willing to receive need to learn to serve. Those who are willing to serve need to learn to receive.

Our "love and good deeds" may be directed toward those within the church but there seems to be s special blessing in focusing service toward the displaced, the marginal and the poor. Taking Jesus's teaching about the sheep and the goats at face value, all Christians may be held accountable to service to others where we actually feed the hungry, welcome a stranger into our life, clothe those who have little, care for someone who is sick, or visit one who is in prison (Mt. 25:31f). Blue collar spirituality challenges us all to get our hands dirty for our own good. We grow in Christ as Christ meets us through those we serve. We meet Christ in "the least of these" (Mt. 25;40).

Andrew Purves believes that a primary fact about compassion is that "compassion means ministry." Compassion is "an action word, a verb...a hands on ministry."[54] For discipleship we must be given a specific ministry, we must do something good in the name of Jesus. This good work is not our own but a result of our relationship with Christ. Purves writes, "Prayer without compassion leads to piety; compassion without prayer leads to pity."[55]

CHAPTER III

A CONGREGATIONAL WORSHIP AND MENTORING PLAN
FOR THE INITIATION OF NEW CHRISTIANS

The Period and Service of Welcome

A. A Theological Review of the Period of Welcome

The period of welcome is a time of beginnings, of invitations and introductions, a time to practice hospitality. Although some may be more blessed with the gift of hospitality than others, we cannot be excused from this important ministry by thinking poorly about ourselves. "Be hospitable to one another without complaining. Like good stewards of the grace of God, serve one another with whatever gift each of you has received" (1 Peter 4:9-10).

At the beginning spiritual companions are strangers. They are just becoming acquainted with the church, with sponsors, with God. We welcome these strangers as guests. We are God's welcome to them. God can do no better for God has given us this ministry of hospitality.

Paul urges us to "extend hospitality to strangers" (Rom. 12:13). Hospitality is an expression of God's love, a form of service to Christ. It is a significant form of being a witness to Christ. Hospitality is an expression of generosity, one of the qualifications for being a leader in the church (1 Tim. 3:2). Hospitality is a form of Christ's love. Love demands a welcome. If we do not welcome, we do not love. If we are not welcomed, we are not loved. Hospitality is a spirituality of beginnings for here lie the seeds for future trust. Mentors practice hospitality whereby we extend to another the welcome of God. Hospitality is an open door, an open heart and an open mind through which another may enter to encounter God.

Susanne Johnson writes that hospitality "is the creation of an environment or space where the stranger is welcomed and received as gift, blessing, and fellow creature, rather than treated as a threat, intruder or annoyance."[56] We may be asked to welcome another whom we care for, perhaps a sinner or an enemy. With God's grace we can be so bold as to be hospitable to all.

Sponsors practice a form of "Mennonite your Way." In this case we are offering others our attention, our hands, our ears rather than our houses. They are on a journey and they are welcome to be with us. This community may prove to be a most important relationship for here God is at work transforming strangers into friends, turning xenophobia into philadelphia. In the Mennonite church, especially in an urban context, we must learn to welcome the stranger.

We should not think that our own hospitality is strong enough to break down the powers of fear and distrust. It is the hospitality of God, the power of God's story, God's welcome in Jesus Christ that is at work in our welcome. When we welcome the stranger, we welcome them in the name of Jesus Christ. If they begin to accept us, they are introduced to Jesus and begin to accept Him.

When we welcome the stranger, we welcome Christ. Jesus said, "I was a stranger and you welcomed me" (Matt. 25:35). What we do to the stranger, we do to Jesus. And for all we know, the ones we welcome, our spiritual companions, may turn out to be "angels" (Heb. 13:1-2). They bring Christ to us as much as we bring Christ to them.

This is a time for beginnings, for opening doors. We can welcome these persons, their past life, their way of thinking. This is a time for acceptance, not rejection, and a time for mercy, not judgment. This is a time to listen rather than argue and debate, a time for smiles and open hands rather than frowns and pointing fingers. This is a time to practice patience and tolerance rather than to fight over words and contend for the faith.

This is a time for sharing stories, a time to listen. We can listen to their spiritual life journey. We can listen to their pain, their shame, their dreams, their felt needs. We can listen for the presence of God for surely God was at work in their life before we arrived on the scene.

This is a time to exercise faith in God. We can learn to trust God to use us as a witness. We do not need to be in a hurry. Let us begin by walking to the pace of our companion. We can rest, relax, be quiet. We can learn to practice holding our tongues and opening our ears. Here we are, giving quiet attention to our companions. This attention may do more to welcome them into the presence of God than any words we can say.

This is a time for sharing the gospel, for telling stories from the scriptures and our own experience that give witness to Christ. This is a time for questions more than answers. We can allow for a searching faith, for doubt and uncertainty, for some confusion in both ourselves and our companions. We do not urgently need to fix them, heal them, to solve their problems or rescue them from hell. That is God's responsibility. For now, all God is asking is that we welcome them in the name of Jesus Christ.

We are also at the beginning of a possible conversion experience, a transformation. We are living in God's time, not our own. Things do not always happen in sequence, according to our plan. We do not need to worry that they may die before we see them again. We are God's letter of invitation that invites another to come and see the presence of God in our life together, in the Word and Sacraments, in the prayers and fellowship of the people.

While in prison, the apostle Paul was given an opportunity to
share the gospel with King Agrippa and his "sister" Bernice. Paul shared
with them his spiritual journey, his conversion experience, the death and
resurrection of Jesus. Festus, the governor of Judea, was also present.
When Paul said that Jesus was the "first to rise from the dead" (Acts
26:23), Festus told Paul he was insane. Paul says that he is "speaking the
sober truth."

> King Agrippa, do you believe the prophets? I know
> that you believe." Agrippa said to Paul, "Are you so
> quickly persuading me to become a Christian?" Paul
> replied, "Whether quickly or not, I pray to God that
> not only you but also all who are listening to me
> today might become such as I am. (Acts 26:27-28).

Not everyone we welcome in the name of Jesus will go on to
become a Christian. We do our best and we know that our best is
acceptable to God. Let us be faithful to our friends in extending to them
the hospitality of God.

B. A Service of Welcome

Receiving of Candidates

> (The candidates and sponsors gather outside the meeting place.
> An elder from the congregation greets each person, conveying
> to them a sense of joy and celebration. He/she invites the
> sponsors and candidates to enter the meeting and to take their
> places in pairs toward the front of the assembly. While they
> enter the congregation sings.)

> Song: Good Morning, Jesus (Cry Hosanna, 21)

> The leader welcomes each candidate by name. "_____, we
> welcome you in the name of Jesus Christ."

> With expression, someone recites Psalm 63:1-4.

Congregational Song: Come and See
                          Hymnal: A Worship Book, 20)
Opening Dialogue

> The leader calls each candidate by name, asking each the
> following questions that they are to answer in their own words.
> These questions were presented to the candidates beforehand

and with the help of their sponsors they have prepared a response.

Leader: What do you ask of God?
Candidate: Eternal life (or another suitable response).
Leader: What do you ask of God's church?
Candidate: Love (or another suitable response).

Presentation and Acceptance of the Gospel

Leader: "This is eternal life, that they may know you, the only true God, and Jesus Christ whom you have sent" (John 17:3). Do you want to be a disciple of Jesus Christ, to follow Jesus in life, seeking to walk in the power of his resurrection?
Candidates: I do
Leader: Is the church of Jesus Christ ready to help these friends to serve and follow Jesus in life?
Sponsors and congregation: We are.
(With hands joined or raised, the leader prays:)
            God of mercy,
            we thank you for these your servants.
            You have sought and summoned them in many ways
            and they have turned to seek you.
            You have called them today
            and they have answered in our presence.
            We praise you, Lord, and we bless you.

Congregational Song: We praise thee, O God"
                    (Hymnal: A Worship Book, 99)

Signing of the Candidates
            The candidates and their sponsors are invited to come forward to receive a sign of God's blessing. In this service of prayer the image of Christ is figuratively stamped upon the heart and mind of the candidate, being a sign that we belong to God. As each of the senses is being signed the sponsors will gently touch the candidate's sense with their hand.

While the head is being signed:
Leader: Receive the touch of Christ upon your mind.
            It is Christ himself who now strengthens you
            with this sign of his love.
            Learn to know the mind of Christ.

Congregation: Christ will be your strength.

While the ears are being signed:

Leader: Receive the touch of Christ upon your ears
           that you may hear the word of God
           Learn to know and hear Christ.

           Congregation: Christ will be your strength.

While the eyes are being signed:

Leader: Receive the touch of Christ upon your eyes
           that you may see the glory of God.
           Learn to know and see Christ in life.
           Congregation: Christ will be your strength.
           While the lips are being signed:
Leader: Receive the touch of Christ upon your lips that you may
           respond to the word of God.
           Learn to know and follow him.
Congregation: Christ will be your strength.

While the heart is being signed:

Leader: Receive the touch of Christ upon your heart
           that Christ may dwell there by faith.
           Learn to know and follow him.
Congregation: Christ will be your strength.

While the shoulders are being signed:

Leader: Receive the touch of Christ upon your shoulder that you may
           bear the gentle yoke of Christ. Learn to know and follow
           him.
Congregation: Christ will be your strength.

While the hands are being signed:

Leader: Receive the touch of Christ on your hands that Christ may be
           known in the work you do. Learn to know and work with
           Christ.
Congregation: Christ will be your strength.

While the feet are being signed:

Leader: Receive the touch of Christ upon your feet that you may walk
           in the way of peace. Learn to know the peace of Christ.
Congregation: Christ will be your strength.

Leader: Let us pray:
>God be in my head
>>and in my understanding;
>God be in my eyes
>>and in my looking;
>God be in my mouth
>>and in my speaking;
>God be in my heart
>>and in my thinking;
>God be at my end
>>and at my departing. AMEN
>(Hymnal: A Worship Book, 738)

Congregational Hymn: Will you let me be your servant
>>(Hymnal: A Worship Book, 307.)

Ministry of the Word

New Testament Reading: John 1:35-42, 1:17b.
Teaching: Come and See Jesus full of Grace and Truth
>Salutations! In the name of Jesus Christ we extend to you God's invitation to come to know God through Jesus Christ. We bear witness that Jesus Christ is the light of the world. "To all who receive him, who believe in his name, he gives power to become children of God" (vs. 12).

I.   In the name of Jesus we invite you to:

>A. Come and Hear the Word of God that was made flesh in Jesus. "Jesus...full of grace and truth" (14,17)
>B. Come and See the glory of God in Jesus. "The Word of God became flesh and lived among us, and we have seen his glory" (vs. 14).
>C. Come and Know God in Jesus Christ. "No one has ever seen God. It is God the only Son, who is close to the Father's heart, who has made him known" (18)
>D. Come and Seek Jesus, the Lamb of God (vs.29-35) who takes away the world's sin and gives the Spirit.

>IF YOU WANT TO SEE GOD, LOOK AT JESUS CHRIST.

II. Jesus speaks to those who begin to believe

>A. "What are you looking for?" (vs. 35-38)
>- What is the hunger, the thirst, the desire, the pain, the dream. Do we seek God?

B. "Come and See" (vs. 39-46).
   - "Where are you staying?" Trust begins with simple questions like "where do you live?"
   - the invitation to a beginning faith: Come, See, and Follow me.
C. "We have found the Messiah" (vs.41).
   - Andrew introduces Peter to Jesus. We can never foresee when we bring another to Jesus what Jesus will make of them.
D. "Can anything good come out of Nazareth?" (vs.46)
E. "Where did you get to know me?" (vs.48)
F. Come and see "the heavens opened" (vs.51).

Ministry of Prayer

Leader: A brief prayer that each person would in all ways grow up in Jesus Christ.

Prayers of the sponsors and the community:
           (Each sponsor is to share a prayer they have prepared for their companion. While they are praying it would be appropriate for them to lay their hands on the shoulder of their companion.)
Leader: Almighty God,
           in whom we live and move and have our being,
           you have made us for yourself,
           so that our hearts are restless
           until they rest in you.
           Grant us purity of heart and strength of purpose,
           that no selfish passion may hinder us
           from knowing your will,
           no weakness from doing it
           but that in your light we may see light clearly,
           and in your service find our perfect freedom,
           through Jesus Christ, our Lord.
           AMEN   (Hymnal: A Worship Book, 737)

Ministry of fellowship

Congregational Sharing: An opportunity to share.
Presentation of Gifts: A home made loaf of bread.
Congregational Hymn: You shall go out with joy
                      (Hymnal: A Worship Book, 427)

The Period and Service of Decision

A. A Theological Review of the Period of Decision

In the RCIA the Rite of Election or Enrollment of Names is celebrated on the first Sunday of Lent. The rite "ratifies the catechumen's readiness for the sacraments of initiation." [54] The rite is composed of five parts: (1) the homily, (2) the presentation of the candidates, (3) the examination of the candidates, (4) the act of admission, and (5) intercession and prayer for the elect. The rite examines the candidates' decision to follow Jesus and impresses upon all who are gathered that we are Christian because of God's choice. God is for us and we are for God.

The Service of Election can be viewed from two viewpoints. On the one hand, as we look to the past, the focus is upon God's choice, the divine initiative. We see in Jesus Christ that God is for us. On the other hand, when we look at the present moment, the focus is upon the human response to the call of God. Are we for God? And when we look to the future, we join hands with others, working together with God, to do the work we are chosen to do.

In this service God is at work discipling people through the community and the Word. The community and the Word of God become instruments of grace that are used to set in place the foundation stone of Christ. The community speaks forth the creative Word of God and holds those who are seeking to follow Jesus accountable to the Word. God is for us. Are we for God? We want to do our best to give attention to the Word, that the Word would conceive and bring forth new life. This meeting can be seen as a transitional moment, an event that may serve to mark the beginning of conversion. This meeting is a symbol of the beginning of a new life in Jesus Christ. The participants are named Christian and the community celebrates the new birth from above. This meeting can serve to testify that these people have welcomed Jesus Christ as their personal Lord and Savior. They have begun the journey of being "chosen out of the world" (John 15:19), and being bonded into the family of God. May God infuse the power of grace and holiness into our being, awaken us to hear God's Word and bond us into the community of Christ.

In some churches there is no celebration marking the beginning of conversion. Conversion is a process that has no beginning, a creation without a big bang. In some traditions the decision to follow Christ is marked by raising the hand or walking the aisle. In the Service of Election the Christian community affirms and celebrates the conception of the life of God in these companions, giving attention to both divine initiative and human response.

The Divine Initiative - God is For Us

> For you are a people holy to the Lord your God; the Lord
> your God has chosen you out of all the peoples on the earth
> to be his people, his treasured possession. (Deut. 7:6)

Just as God chose Israel, God has chosen us to be God's
treasured possession.   The Service of Election is designed to enable
people to give attention to their election in Christ. God is a seeking and
speaking God. Jesus told his friends, "You did not choose me but I
chose you" (John 15:16). This period of time provides an opportunity for
people to hear and respond to God's call, like when God called Samuel
and Samuel responded, "Here I am Lord,..Speak, for your servant is
listening" (1 Sam. 3:4,10b).

This service is a way of making meaning of the reality of our
election in Jesus Christ.   This event can build assurance and
appreciation, acting to "confirm (our) call and election" (2 Pet. 1:10).
Our name is written in the "book of life" (Luke 10:20, Phil 4:3). God calls
us by name, we belong to God, we are precious and loved by God (Isa.
43:1,4). "(God) has chosen you and not cast you off" (Isa. 41:9b). Our
name is on the list. We belong.

> Peter, an apostle of Jesus Christ, To the exiles of
> the Dispersion...who have been chosen and
> destined by God the Father and sanctified by the
> Spirit to be obedient to Jesus Christ and to be
> sprinkled with his blood: May grace and peace be
> yours in abundance (1 Pet. 1:1-2).

There are four aspects of election in the preceding verses.
First, we are "chosen and destined by God." Election is not a human
invention but a divine revelation. Because of God's call upon our lives
we are separated from the world, "called out of the world" (John 15:19).
We are chosen to live in nonconformity with the world.

Second, we are elected to holiness. We have been chosen by
God to be a holy people, made holy by the Spirit. Paul writes, "(God)
chose us in Christ, before the foundation of the world to be holy and
blameless before him in love" (Eph.1:4).   Election is an incentive to
holiness, not an excuse for sin.

Third, we are chosen and sanctified by the Spirit "to be
obedient to Jesus Christ." We are elected to obey, not to play. As Jesus
said, "You did not choose me but I chose you. And I appointed you to
go and bear fruit, fruit that will last" (John 15:16). The purpose of our
election in Christ is to live a holy life, to be obedient to Jesus, to do the
will of God, to bear fruit, to work together with Christ. We are elected
to obedience and service.

Fourth, people are to be "sprinkled with his blood." Peter is referring to the example of Moses who ratified the covenant God established at Mount Sinai by building an altar and making a burnt offering to God. As the covenant was read, the people would say, "All that the Lord has spoken we will do, and we will be obedient" (Ex. 24:7). As they spoke Moses "dashed the blood on the people" (v.8). This was a symbolic act of dedication, binding the people to obey the covenant. Just as Moses dashed the blood of the sacrifice over the people, ratifying God's covenant with them, reminding the people of their promise of obedience, so the Service of Election can serve to ratify God's new covenant through the blood of Christ and remind us of our call to nonconformity, holiness and obedience. We are using liturgical action to help effect an ethical lifestyle. The symbolic action can serve to remind us that Christians are called to obey and even to suffer for Christ.[58]

The Service of Election can act to call people to active duty. This meeting can serve to mark the time of our ordination, our call to ministry. Here is a time when the ordinary saint is blessed, chosen, named, and called to live a holy and obedient life as a servant of Jesus Christ.

The Service of Election is not a service of perfection. It is a ceremony in which we are aware that we are chosen by God as imperfect people. It is not an award ceremony celebrating human accomplishments but a service conferring upon people the blessings of God.

During this meeting people may become aware of weakness. We respond to God's call as did Moses, Isaiah, Jeremiah. We do not feel qualified, holy, or able to do what God is calling forth in our lives. We can balk at the thought of being a holy person. A sense of vulnerability and inadequacy is good. We are truly being called to be and to do what is beyond our own ability. Only with God's grace are holiness and obedience possible. In the world people are elected and chosen because of wisdom, power, wealth, superior talent and ability. With God things are different. Pride obstructs and disqualifies us from the recognition of God's blessing. Paul writes,

> Consider your own call, brothers and sisters: not many of you were wise by human standards, not many were powerful, not many were of noble birth. But God chose what is foolish in the world to shame the strong; God chose what is low and despised in the world, things that are not, to reduce to nothing things that are, so that no one might boast in the presence of God (1 Cor. 1:26-29).

God often chooses the plain and the simple. The inadequacy we may feel need not prevent us from following Jesus. An awareness of our poverty of spirit, our weakness, our need for God is a key that opens our ears and hearts to hear and receive God's blessing. The Service of Election may help people to let go of a poor self-concept and to identify their true self in Christ.

In this meeting we can experience the blessing that is ours in Christ. We stand before God with the freedom to speak. "...we have boldness before God, and we receive from him whatever we ask, because we obey his commandments and what pleases him" (1 John 3:21,22). Hans Urs von Balthasar writes,

> This parrhesia on our part is the open, unconstrained and childlike approach to the Father, neither ashamed nor fearing shame. We come to him with heads held high, as those who have an innate right to be there and speak. We may look into the Father's face without fear...The door stands open, and wherever the child of God may be, there too is that open door. Man is not the door; it is Christ,...[59]

Our election in Christ is not an abstract idea, an argument, a mental prescription that seeks only to explain the mystery of God's sovereign grace. Our election in Christ describes the experience of being chosen by God for no other reason except for the love of God. It is the experience of standing before God with the boldness that comes through faith in Jesus Christ. Election describes the religious experience of encountering God. It is the experience of being loved unconditionally. Election describes the experience of being chosen, loved and ordained by God. The Service of Election is formational and informational. We are in the realm of adoration, not speculation, praise rather than precision. We come before God as children, not as scholars and experts. Election is a parent-child relationship, the language of the heart, the word of love that we long to hear.

Some Christians are unsure of their calling. We are embedded in a culture which is characterized by a sense of rejection. Rather than feeling chosen many people feel homeless, "orphaned."[60] People feel cursed rather then blessed, abandoned and overlooked. God's grace must be given an opportunity to speak to this sense of rejection. The experience of our election in Jesus Christ is an antidote for this sense of rejection. Those who are abandoned are addressed by the Word and the community of God as "chosen," "dearly loved," God's treasure," "holy and chosen one." Their names are written in the "Book of Life." We are all reminded that we are "strangers no more," we are accepted in Christ, not rejected or thrown out but embraced. The Word of God can speak to loneliness and emptiness. Loved, accepted, welcomed, named, chosen, we are now less prone to submit to the addictions and idols of our age.

These ceremonies are alternative rituals of connection that may act to displace the rituals of isolation that seem to dominate our lives. T.V., the movies, shopping, drugs and alcohol, sports and fitness, food, the weekend escape, work. The Service of Election becomes a transformational moment, providing meaning and God's power to grow.

The Human Response - We are for God

Jesus asked his disciples to ratify their initial decision to follow him. After they had become acquainted with Jesus and his teaching, Jesus asked his disciples whether they would continue with him or leave. After counting the cost would they continue to abide in Jesus or would they leave? Jesus examined his disciples to see if their initial decision to follow him was authentic. The Service of Election is a time for decision, to ensure that those who initially decide to follow Jesus desire to continue. People who begin to follow Jesus do not always continue. Many who initially responded positively to the word of the gospel later decided they did not want to go on with Jesus. Jesus said of them that they "fell away" (Matt. 13:21). The Parable of the Sower is about people who responded positively to the gospel. Some of them bear fruit while others do not. Those who bear no fruit fall away because "they have no root", or because they encounter "trouble" or "persecution,' or the "lure of wealth." The Service of Election is designed to examine the resolve of those who are seeking to follow Christ.

Jesus said, "Whoever does not carry the cross and follow me cannot be my disciple" (Luke 14:27). Jesus knew that those who would follow him would suffer. Only those who are willing to suffer will follow, the rest will leave.

Jesus said, "Very truly, I tell you, unless you eat the flesh of the Son of Man and drink his blood, you have no life in you" (John 6:53). Many of the disciples found this teaching difficult to accept. John writes that as a result of this teaching "...many of his disciples turned back and no longer went about with him" (John 6:66). They turned back because they were unwilling to suffer.[61] Jesus asked the twelve, "Do you also wish to go away?" Peter responded, "We have come to believe and know that you are the Holy One of God" (John 6:69).

Just as Jesus asked his disciples, "Do you also wish to go away?", we ask those who seek baptism into Christ and the church whether they are sure they desire to go on with Jesus. The Service of Election provides an opportunity to practice the discipline of accountability. Those seeking baptism into Christ and the church are asked if their conversion is authentic. After coming to believe and know

Jesus, after becoming acquainted with the strengths and weaknesses of the church community, after encountering struggle and beginning to recognize the cost of discipleship are they still willing to follow Jesus?

The Service of Election is a moment of decision. It protects and implements the voluntaristic principle of the believers' church. It provides an occasion for adult converts who may have experienced a conversion event to name this event. It also provides an occasion for children who have grown up in the Christian community to name their conversion.   The church must speak up front about the cost of discipleship, that a decision to follow Christ means that we are called to suffer for Jesus.

> For to this you have been called, because Christ
> also suffered for you, leaving you an example, so
> that you should follow in his steps (1 Pet. 2:21).

In this Service of Election those seeking baptism into Christ and the church are asked if they are sincere in their faith in Christ. Do they truly want to be a committed participant in this church? Their sponsor is to give witness to their commitment, testifying to the sincerity of their faith, promising the support of the church to walk with them on their spiritual journey.

B. The Service of Decision

Call to Worship

Praise and Worship: Lord, I want to be a Christian
                                        (Hymnal: A Worship Book, 444)

Time of Election - God is for us!

Leader: Those who are being called by God to be baptized and become members of this church please come forward with your sponsor as your names are called. (The companions and their friends gather in the front of the meeting place, facing each other.)
Leader: Let us hear the Word of the Lord.
Reader: "Grace to you and peace. We always give thanks to God for all of you and mention you in our prayers,... For we know, brothers and sisters beloved by God, that he has chosen you,..." (1 Thessalonians 1:2,4)
Leader: God has chosen you and wants you to know the joy of belonging to God's family. We want you to know that you are loved and chosen by God.

Companions: Speaking to their friend they say to them,
        "You are loved and chosen by God."
Reader: "...thus says the Lord, he who created you,... Do not fear, for I
        have redeemed you; I have called you by name, you are mine."
        (Isa. 43:1)
Leader: The people of God want you to know that God has called you
        by name, you belong to God.
Companions: Speaking their friend's name, they say
        "_____, you belong to God."
Reader: Jesus said, "You did not choose me but I chose you. And I
        appointed you to go and bear fruit, fruit that will last, so that
        the Father will give you whatever you ask him in my name"
        (John 15:16).
Leader: The people of God want you to know that Jesus has chosen you
        to bear fruit that will last.
Companions: "Jesus has chosen you to bear fruit that will last."
Reader: "For you are a people holy to the Lord your God, the Lord your
        God has chosen you out of all the peoples on earth to be his
        people, his treasured possession" (Deuteronomy 7:6).
Leader: The people of God want you to know that you are God's
        treasured possession.
Companions: "You are God's treasured possession."

Congregational Song: God has called you, God will not fail you.

Minstrel serenade: I sought the Lord
        Hymnal: A Worship Book, 506)

Ministry of the Word

Scripture Reading: Reader, 1 Peter 1:1-2

Teaching: 1 Peter 1:1-2
        A. To exiles of the dispersion
        B. Chosen by God
        C. Chosen by God to live a holy life
        D. Chosen by God to be obedient to Jesus Christ
        E. A sign of our Election
        (as a sign of our being chosen by God, water could be gently
        splashed upon the candidates and the congregation during the
        following song)

Congregational Song: Lord, you have come to the lakeshore
        (Hymnal: A Worship Book, 229)

Time for Decision - We are for God!

Leader: Who do you say that Jesus is?
Seeker: (Each companion will respond for himself/herself)
Leader: Do you confess with your lips that Jesus is Lord and believe in your heart that God raised him from the dead?
Seeker: (Together, the companions respond, Yes.)
Reader: Jesus said, "If any want to become my followers, let them deny themselves and take up their cross and follow me" (Mark 8:34).
Leader: Are you willing to live a holy and obedient life, to be a minister of Jesus Christ?
Seeker: Yes.
Leader: Are you willing to suffer for Jesus?
Seeker: Yes.
Leader: At this time the sponsors will provide witness to the seekers' faith in Christ. [Sponsors]
Leader: As a sign that you are Christians and that you are welcome in God's family, we invite you to come forward when your name is called. Believe that your name is written in the Book of Life.

Congregational Song: Written in the Book of Life

Prayers of Thanksgiving (Congregation to stand)

Leader: We are grateful to God, that God has blessed us in Jesus Christ with every spiritual blessing, let us give praise to God:
People: Praise the Lord!
Leader: That our names are written in the Book of Life, let us give praise to God:
People: Praise the Lord!!
Leader: That God has chosen us in Christ before the foundation of the world to be holy and blameless before him in love, let us give praise to God:
People: Praise the Lord!!!
Leader: That we are a chosen people, a royal priesthood, God's own people, that we belong to the family of God, let us give praise to God:
People: Praise the Lord!!!!
Leader: That Jesus Christ has chosen us to bear fruit that will last, let us give praise to God:
People: Praise the Lord!!!!!
Leader: That these people who come before us this day have called on the name of the Lord Jesus Christ and they have salvation, let us give praise to God:
People: Praise the Lord!!!!!!

Congregational Song: I have decided to follow Jesus.

Prayers of Intercession

Leader: We have been chosen by God to live a new life, to walk together in the power of the resurrection of Christ. Let us pray to the Lord.
People: Lord, hear our prayer.
Leader: That you would enable us to faithfully lead them to you, let us pray to the Lord:
People: Lord, hear our prayer.
Leader: That their families and friends would not put obstacles in their way but would see Christ in them and come to know you as their Lord and Savior, let us pray to the Lord:
People: Lord, hear our prayer.
Leader: That we would all find joy in daily prayer, let us pray to the Lord:
People: Lord, hear our prayer.
Leader: that we may grow up and grow together in Christ.
People: Lord, hear our prayer.
Leader: That your Word would abide in us, and that your Word would give birth to love, truth, justice and peace, let us pray to the Lord:
People: Lord, hear our prayer.
Leader: That we would humbly acknowledge our faults and work together to correct them, let us pray to the Lord:
People: Lord, hear our prayer.
Leader: That we may be willing to share with another your love and joy, let us pray to the Lord:
People: Lord, hear our prayer.
Leader: That you would enable us to obey you and to serve you, let us pray to the Lord:
People: Lord, hear our prayer. AMEN

Benediction (or a concluding hymn)
    Lord God,
    you created the human race
    and are the author of its renewal.
    Bless all your adopted children
    add these chosen ones
    to the harvest of your new covenant.
    As true children of the promise,
    may they rejoice in eternal life,
    won, not by the power of nature,
    but through the mystery of your grace. Amen.
    We ask this through Christ our Lord. (RCIA, 74)

The Period and Service of Purification and Enlightenment

A.   A Theological Review of the Period of Purification and Enlightenment

In the RCIA, the period of purification and enlightenment corresponds to the time of Lent. This is a time for reflection and repentance in which the mind and the heart are purified and enlightened with a deeper knowledge of Christ. During this season of Lent the companions may participate in three services called "Scrutinies" and one service named "Presentations." The Scrutinies "are meant to uncover, then heal, all that is weak, defective, or sinful in the hearts of the elect; to bring out, then strengthen all that is upright, strong, and good."[59] They are celebrated "in order to deliver the elect from the power of sin and Satan, to protect them against temptation, and to give them strength in Christ, who is the way, the truth, and the life."[60] The Presentation is a ceremony in which the elect are entrusted with the Creed and the Lord's Prayer, both of which they are to commit to memory.

During the forty days of Lent the church enters into a period of examination and testing. In the school of Christ, there is a time for testing just as in any school. Paul writes, "Examine yourselves to see whether you are living in the faith. Test yourselves" (2 Cor.13:5). This is a time of cleansing as in the forty days and nights of rain that purged the earth of sin in the days of Noah. This is a time of testing and deliverance as in the forty years Israel spent in the desert being set free from the slavery to Egypt and idols. This is a time of preparation and testing like the forty days Jesus spent in the desert preparing for the journey ahead. This is a spirituality of the desert, a spirituality of winter. Before the new growth, the seed lies dormant in the frozen soil.

This time of examination is meant to hold us accountable for growth in Christ. It is a time for naming and confessing our sins, for binding and loosing, for naming and exorcising evil. This period provides us an opportunity to examine our weakness and strength. Where are we wounded? Where are we healthy?   What needs protection? What obstacles to growth exist? For what do we hunger and thirst? How are we being asked to change? What resistance to change is occurring? What sacrifice is God calling forth in our life? What temptation do we struggle with? This time of examination is not meant to fail us but to expose our weakness and strength, preparing the companions for baptism, the church for Easter and spring.

In adapting this paradigm to the Mennonite church, we will focus on the disciplines of suffering, confession, forgiveness, and deliverance. This is an appropriate time to practice self-denial, to bear our cross and to be attentive to suffering.   Through deliverance, confession and forgiveness, the work of suffering, God is present to purify and enlighten our lives and to prepare us for ministry.

Suffering and Sacrifice

Jesus told his disciples that he would undergo great suffering, be killed, and then he would rise again. He then warned his disciples that they would also suffer. He said,

> If any want to become my followers, let them deny themselves and take up their cross and follow me. For those who want to save their life will lose it, and those who lose their life for my sake, and for the sake of the gospel, will save it (Mark 8:34,35).

If the leader suffers, so will those who follow the leader. If we follow Christ, suffering is inevitable. Christians need to be warned that things are going to get worse before things get better and heaven arrives. The journey is going to be difficult. This does not mean that we invite or choose suffering, but that when suffering occurs we will be prepared for it. We do not will to suffer but we are willing to suffer for Christ and the sake of the gospel. The point is if we choose to follow Christ, we will experience an increase of suffering.

Basil Pennington writes that the Russian Christian prays to be able to bear the cross well. The Greek Orthodox Christian, when the cross comes, prays for immediate deliverance.[64]

One is not better than the other. We should be able to go both ways. Christ is not more bitter than sweet, but bitter-sweet. When suffering comes to us we can pray with Jesus, "My Father, if it is possible, let this cup pass from me" (Matt. 26:39). If we are not delivered and must walk the hard way, then we pray with Jesus, "...not what I want but what you want" (Matt. 26:39). We pray asking God to give us the strength to persevere.

When it is the will of God that we suffer there can be no substitute for the way of the cross. The avoidance of suffering is neurosis.[65] The avoidance of suffering gives birth to addiction.[66] Religion can be used as a substitute for suffering. Rather than escape the suffering that will occur because we follow Jesus, we must be willing to bear it. Dorothee Soelle says that today's Jesus is "a stranger to pain."[67] Jesus reveals to us a God who suffers, who is acquainted with pain.

If the sufferings of Christ are abundant, so is our consolation (2 Cor. 1:5). When Jesus was drafting his disciples, he was warning them that they might die in battle as he would. But after death, God would raise him up. The historical fact of the resurrection of Christ enables the disciples to suffer and risk their lives for the sake of Christ and the gospel. If there is no resurrection, then self-denial, sacrifice, and bearing the cross are foolish. If people are willing to die in battle for the sake of land with no hope of resurrection, then how much more can we be willing to suffer for the sake of Christ with the hope of the resurrection.

Self-denial is sacrifice. It is not self-hatred but a willingness to offer up the treasure of one's self for God's purpose. Science, the military, agriculture, medicine make this same kind of demand for self-denial. If you are going to be a doctor you will be warned and asked to deny yourself for the sake of medicine. As a Christian we are told that we must be willing to offer to Christ our self as a living sacrifice, as our service to God (Rom. 12:1). We give our self to God as God has given God's self to us. Christ suffered and died for us and we may be called upon to suffer and die for the purpose of God.

That suffering is our destiny is clear in the scripture. When Paul was chosen to carry the name of Christ to the Gentiles Jesus said, "I myself will show him how much he must suffer for the sake of my name" (Acts 9:10). Paul's experience bears this out. He wrote, "We were so utterly, unbearably crushed that we despaired of life itself" (2 Cor. 1:8). He said to Timothy, "Indeed, all who want to live a godly life in Christ Jesus will be persecuted" (2 Tim. 3:12). Just as soldiers are prepared to suffer, Timothy is told, "Share in suffering like a good soldier of Jesus Christ" (2 Tim. 2:3). To the Philippians he said that God has "graciously granted you the privilege of not only believing in Christ, but of suffering for him as well" (Phil. 1:9). Paul and Barnabas asserted that "it is through many persecutions that we must enter the kingdom of God" (Acts 14:22). Peter wrote,

> For to this you have been called, because Christ also suffered for you, leaving you an example, so that you should follow in his steps....When he was abused, he did not return abuse; when he suffered, he did not threaten; but he entrusted himself to the one who judges justly. He himself bore our sins in his body on the cross, so that, free form sins, we might live for righteousness; by his wounds you have been healed. For you were going astray like sheep, but now you have returned to the shepherd and guardian of your souls (1 Peter 2:21-25).

We will follow the example of Christ. Just as he suffered, so shall we. Yet, as we follow Christ, we will find our many wounds healed by his wounds. Having gone astray we have been returned by Christ to the guardian of our souls. All our sins he bore on the cross. Now we are free to live for righteousness. Healed, returned to God, free, forgiven, blessed we no longer return abuse for abuse. We no longer make threats when we suffer. From now on we learn to entrust our self to God. From now on we will "do right and suffer for it" (1

Peter 2;20). Having the mind of Christ we will humble ourselves in obedience to God, trusting in God to defend and deliver us.

Suffering may be redemptive, a way God may use to enable us to become mature Christians. Mennonite John Oyer writes that suffering is "useful and necessary to strengthen and purify the Christian."[68] Presbyterian Andrew Purves says that "suffering...was understood by Jesus to be a constitutive part of discipleship."[69] Even Christ was made "perfect through suffering" (Heb. 2:10). Even Christ "learned obedience through what he suffered" (Heb. 5:8). Some things we learn, some things are changed, only through the crisis of suffering. Some sins we leave behind only through the process of suffering (1 Peter 4:1,2).

Through suffering God is at work purifying and enlightening our minds and heart, our church, our world. Suffering is a divine medicine through which we are healed and made holy. Suffering is a way God may use to break us of our addictions, idolatry, and attachment to the values of the world. Suffering is a spiritual discipline in which God is at work for good "so that we may share in (God's) holiness" (Heb. 12:10). Suffering is a means by which God builds our Christian character (Rom. 5:3,4). Our warfare and violence often end only when the quota of suffering is full. We do not seek the cross but when it is our turn to suffer let us pray God will give us the grace to persevere.

In self-denial we give up control of our own destiny. We let go of being in charge of our own lives. We are willing to "lose our lives" for the sake of Jesus. We are open to say "no" to our own plans and ambitions. We yield our self to the will of God rather than insist on our own way. We let go of an egocentric, self-centered, self-defensive existence and surrender our self into the loving and strong hand of God. A narrow definition of the suffering we may be called upon to bear is a form of theological elitism. There is more than one way to suffer for Christ. God may use a jail cell to purify our heart or God may use the loss of our honor to do the same.

This dying to self involves a profound and growing trust in the promise of Christ, a belief in the gospel. God must help us to overcome our fear of dying to self so that we can risk the obedience of faith. This fear of dying is overcome not by our own reason or courage but by looking to Jesus. We see the cross, the humiliation and pain of the bitter Christ. And we see beyond the cross to the exaltation and joy of the sweet Jesus. We see Jesus risen from the dead. There is nothing that we give to God that God will not return.

Peter rebuked Jesus for Jesus' belief in a suffering God. Jesus emphatically tells Peter that Peter is not speaking for God but for Satan. Satan and Peter do not believe in suffering, God does. Peter would later refuse to follow Jesus because he was afraid of dying. His fear of dying is overcome by the resurrection of Christ. If Jesus is risen then we have nothing to fear.

To die to self may mean we lose our job because we refuse to build a weapon for war. It may mean learning to submit to one another, that we do not always need to get our own way. It may mean the experience of giving up our own rights, money, power, time, for the work of God. It may mean facing our imperfections and weakness, dying to unrealistic expectations and false visions of grandeur. We learn to be vulnerable and in our weakness we fine God makes us strong. We grow up in Christ as we confess weakness; we begin with our weakness, not our strength. In spiritual friendship it is better to speak of pain than pride. If everything is laughter and fun I doubt that anything good will come of it. Our lives need the water of tears to grow.

Deliverance

The power of sin and evil is very real. Paul writes that we struggle "against the cosmic powers of this present darkness" (Eph. 6:12). He calls us to be strong in the Lord and to "stand against the wiles of the devil" (Eph. 6:11). Whether we understand these rulers, authorities and cosmic powers as the power of the state, tradition, law, social institutions or as the power of personal, supernatural beings that may misuse structures and institutions for the purpose of evil, we are engaged in a war with evil and sin. War, genocide, racism, abortion, abuse, greed, lust, poverty and oppression are evil. Families are being destroyed, the earth is being damaged, children are dying, violence is so prevalent. People love money. All this represents a real war between the powers of good and evil that begins in the first chapter of Genesis and continues into the last chapter of Revelation.

Human consciousness, our collective resolve, our combined scientific and educational wisdom, our best medicine and politics are no match for these powers of evil. We cannot overcome the powers of sin and evil. We cannot heal or protect ourselves. God must enter the arena and fight for us. God is the one who must "protect us from the evil one" (Matt. 6:13, 2 Thess. 3:3). It is only because God is with us that we can "fear no evil" (Psalm 23:4). Apart from Christ "we can do nothing" (John 15:5). The historical victory of Christ over the powers of evil must be applied to our everyday lives. Where we are in bondage— blind, deaf, dumb—Christ must set us free by his victory over the power of evil. God must fight for us. God must awaken us, lift us up, chase away our fears.

Lent provides us an opportunity to attend to the need for the ministry of deliverance. We name the pain, the powers of evil and sin that afflict us, our churches and our world. We identify what is sick and is diseased. We invite God to cast out all evil, to save us and deliver us from sin. We name the victims and we name the victor; we name the suffering and we name the Savior. We ask God to awaken all who are sleeping, to lift up all who have fallen, to remove all obstacles that hinder us from growth. Our part is to seek God in prayer, to listen to and affirm the story of the victory of Jesus Christ over the powers of hell. Our part is to be defended by the Word of God, to put on the "armor of God." Our part is to depend upon Christ, to ask for help, to seek God. Our part is to humble our self before God, to recognize that we are powerless in the face of evil. We name the demons, the idols, the addictions and sins that consume us. We abandon ourselves into God's care without knowing what God may do. We worship God in the face of adversity and call upon Christ to save us.

Practically, we pray prayers of deliverance and exorcism. We name both the personal and social evil, the sin, the confusion, obstacle, and strife and in the name of Jesus Christ we ask God to cast it out. We speak the Word of God to Satan. We worship Christ, proclaim the gospel, expose the darkness to the light. We pray for our enemies. We pray, "Lord rescue us from evil." "The Lord is faithful; he will strengthen you and protect you from the evil one" (2 Thess. 3:3). We simply pray as Jesus prayed, "Holy Father... protect them from the evil one" (John 17:11,15). "Ephphatha, that is, "Be opened" (Mark 7:34). "Talitha cum", which means, "Little girl, get up!" (Mark 5:41). "Peace! Be still!" (Mark 4:39).

We do not dwell upon the evil, we turn our attention to God. As Bonhoeffer says, "The devil yields to no human attack...Christ must enter the battlefield with his clear word.[70] In worship we declare our allegiance to Christ, together engaging in spiritual warfare, celebrating the victory of Christ over the powers of evil, sin and death. Prayer must precede action. Our God must fight for us.

Confession and Forgiveness

"Confess your sins to one another, and pray for one another, so that you may be healed" (James 5:16). Lent is a fine time to practice confession, that God would take away our sin and purify us from all unrighteousness. We open ourselves to the scrutiny of the Word. What is there that is sinful, weak, defective that God would haul away to the dump? What is there that is closed, blind, deft that needs to be opened by the Word? What idol, addiction, attachment do we need freedom from? What arguments need to end? This is a time to let go of anger and bitterness by giving them to Christ. Where have I refused to love and obey, where am I resisting change? Bonhoeffer believed that specific sins must come to light. "Sin is, in every instance, something quite concrete. It must be recognized and identified by name. Only the demon which is called by name departs."[71]

With regards to the church we can name and confess our corporate sin. Is there a competitive spirit, incivility, spiritual pride, a divided house? Are we spiritually frigid, undisciplined? Confession is good for us. Our part is to practice the discipline of confession, to be truthful, honest, vulnerable, to humble ourselves, to admit we are imperfect. Our part is to make a moral inventory of our life and share it with the Lord and if needed, one other person. We should not spend all our time trying to figure out what, when, where, how, and who to confess to. Often this is just a way for us to avoid the confession. Pray that God will show us the specific way to make confession, whether we confess to God alone, to our spiritual companion, to a small group, to the one we have wronged. Pray that God will provide the right person to hear our confession. Let us bring our sins to the Lamb of God who is the one who "takes away the sin of the world" (John 1:29). Christ takes away our sin and the sin of the world to fill us with the Holy Spirit (John 1:33).

The law of Christ is the law of love. When this law of love is broken there is sin, and the rule of Christ as recorded in Matthew 18 becomes operative. Love must be restored, so we go to our sister or brother for the purpose of reconciliation. The context of Matthew 18 suggests that the central issue Jesus was addressing is the concept of forgiveness. The period of purity and light intentionally encourages the Christian community to practice the discipline of binding and loosing. The point is to forgive.

Confession of sin and the grace of forgiveness prepare the way for the healing presence of Christ. This kind of humility opens the windows of heaven through which God pours upon us the Holy Spirit. Forgiveness means to "let go." We ask God to enable us by God's grace to be made willing to let go of our anger, resentment, hatred, horror. Forgiveness is how God responds to us in Jesus Christ. Through the experience of our own forgiveness we are healed by Christ and enabled to forgive those who have harmed us.

B. The Service of Purification and Enlightenment

Call to Worship

> If I go forward, he is not there;
> or backward, I cannot perceive him;
> on the left he hides, and I cannot behold him;
> I turn to the right, but I cannot see him;
> But he knows the way that I take;
> when he has tested me, I shall come out like gold. (Job 23:8-10)

Songs of Praise and Worship

> I Will Enter His Gates; I Will Call upon the Lord;
> Shine, Jesus, Shine; Wonderful Grace of Jesus

Opening Remarks on Purification and Enlightenment

1. This is a time for confession, repentance and reflection in which our minds and hearts are purified and enlightened with a deeper knowledge of Christ. We want to walk in the light, that God will forgive and cleanse us and our church from our sins (1 John 1:7-9).

2. This is a time we examine ourselves to see whether we are living in the faith (2 Cor. 13:5). We pray that God would be present among us to uncover and heal all that is weak, defective, or sinful, that God would bring out into the light and strengthen all that is good and right. We are the branches God prunes and cleanses that we may bear fruit (John 15:2).

3. This is time for deliverance. We pray that God would protect us from temptation and deliver us, our families, our city, our church, our world, from the powers of evil.

Scripture Reading: Ps. 51

Responsive reading: (*Hymnal, A Worship Book*, 690)

Hymn: Have thine own way (*Hymnal, A Worship Book*, 504)

Teaching: A Man with a Speech Impediment (Mark 7: 32-37), or Raising of Lazarus (John 11:1-45).

Prayers of Intercession

Silent prayer: Let us kneel to express a humble and repentant spirit. Ask that God would purify and enlighten our hearts and our minds. (To end the silence the leader may say) "though our sins are like scarlet, they shall be like snow" (Isa. 1:18).

Prayer for Purification: (Sponsors put your hand upon the shoulder of your companion. Following the words, "we pray in the name of Jesus Christ", the congregation responds, "Lord, hear our prayer.")

Leader: Let us pray for one another that we may remain faithful to Jesus Christ. Lord, we pray that we may be given grace to repent and confess of sin, we pray in the name of Jesus Christ.

People: Lord, hear our prayer.

Leader: When we are in the wilderness with wild animals being tempted by Satan, may you always provide for us a way out, and may angels wait upon us, we pray in the name of Jesus Christ.

People: Lord, hear our prayer.
Leader: Lord, we are willing to have you remove from our lives anything that is displeasing or contrary to you, we pray in the name of Jesus Christ.
People: Lord, hear our prayer.
Leader: We ask that we may know for sure that our sins are forgiven. We ask that we may be given the grace to forgive those who sin against us, we pray in the name of Jesus Christ.
People: Lord, hear our prayer.
Leader: And we pray that whenever you deliver us from evil, that we may always be willing to share with others how much you have done for us, we pray in the name of Jesus Christ.
People: Lord, hear our prayer.
Leader: We ask that you would awaken us, lift us up from all sin, addiction, confusion, violence, guilt, shame, sickness, fear. "TALITHA CUM," we pray in the name of Jesus Christ.
People: Lord, hear our prayer.
Leader: That the Holy Spirit will help us to overcome shame, guilt, fear, pride, and distrust that hinders us from following Jesus. May we hear your words "take heart, and be afraid no more," we pray in the name of Jesus Christ.
People: Lord, hear our prayer.
Leader: That no one will lead us astray, we pray in the name of Jesus Christ.
People: Lord, hear our prayer.
Leader: That when faced with the values of the world we may be conformed to the example of Christ, we pray in the name of Jesus Christ.
People: Lord, hear our prayer.
Leader: That we may all have a horror of sin that distorts our lives, we pray in the name of Jesus Christ.
People: Lord, hear our prayer.
Leader: That we may grow up into Christ in every way, and that our families may put their faith in Christ, we pray in the name of Jesus Christ.
People: Lord, hear our prayer.
Leader: Stand up in the power of Christ and sing.

Hymn: I am weak and I need thy strength O Lord
          (*Hymnal, A Worship Book*, 553)

A Time for Repentance and Confession

A Time for Forgiveness and Deliverance   (Different people can be chosen to pray each sentence.)

1. Lord Jesus, you are the lamb of God who takes away the sin of the world (John 1:29).
2. Your name is Jesus, you save us from our sins (Matthew 1:21).
3. In Jesus Christ, we have redemption, the forgiveness of sins (Colossians 1:20).
4. Christ makes peace through the blood of the cross (Colossians 1:20).
5. We believe that the Son of God was revealed for this purpose, to destroy the works of the devil (1 John 3:8).
6. Father, we call upon you to fight for us, to rescue us from the evil one (Matthew 6:13).
7. I WILL FEAR NO EVIL, FOR YOU ARE WITH ME (Ps.23:4).
8. In the name of Jesus Christ we rebuke and cast out   all unclean spirits (Mark 1:25).
9. We are strong in the Lord and in the strength of his power we put on the whole armor of God so that we may be able to stand against the wiles of the devil (Ephesians 6:10,11).
10. We know, Lord, that you are faithful, that you will strengthen us and guard us from evil (2 Thess.3:3).
11. Defend us from the power of evil, lust, lies, violence, hatred, false values, greed, fear, sickness, death.
12. Protect us from the vain reliance on self.
13. Rule over the spirit of evil that would touch our families, our congregations, our world, by the power of your resurrection from the dead.
14. Tread down the powers of hell.
15. Remove from our lives all obstacles that would keep us from being a holy people. Amen

Ephphatha Ceremony (optional)

Hymn: Breathe on me, breath of God
(*Hymnal, A Worship book*, 356)

(During this hymn the people may be invited to come forward for prayer. Those chosen to pray would recite the following prayer over each person. As they pray they may gently touch the ears and lips of those who are receiving prayer. After they say "Be filled with the Holy Spirit" they may gently blow upon the forehead of the person.)

Ephphatha, that is be opened.
    that your ears may be opened,
    your tongue released,
    that you may speak plainly (Mark 7:34-35).
    Be filled with the Holy Spirit.

Hymn: And I will bear you up on eagles' wings.
          (*Hymnal, A Worship Book,* 596)

The Period and Service of Baptism

A. A Brief Theological Overview of Baptism

1. The Baptism of Jesus

> In those days Jesus...was baptized by John in the Jordan. And just as he was coming up out of the water, he saw the heavens torn apart and the Spirit descending like a dove on him. And a voice came from heaven, "You are my Son, the Beloved; with you I am well pleased" (Mark 1:9-11).

It is reasonable to conclude that Jesus's own baptism became the prototype for Christian baptism. Kilian McDonnell and George Montague write, "The baptism of Jesus structures, orders Christian baptism."[72] The focal point of the baptism of Jesus is the descent of the Holy Spirit. Just as the Spirit came upon Jesus in his baptism, so the Spirit comes upon the Christian in baptism. As demonstrated in Jesus' baptism the essential meaning of Christian baptism is the reception of the gift of the Holy Spirit followed by the affirmation of God's love.

Jesus' own instruction to his companions to make disciples by baptizing them and teaching them (Mt. 28:20) is the creative source for the practice of Christian baptism. We are told by the authoritative word of Jesus to make disciples through the process of teaching and the event of baptism. The baptism of Jesus provides the meaning of baptism, the word of Jesus validates the practice of baptism, and in the service of baptism the sign of the gift of the Holy Spirit is the laying on of hands and prayer.

2. Baptism in Acts

In Acts, water baptism is one event in the story of Christian conversion. James Dunn writes, "The New Testament never uses 'baptism' as a description of the total event of becoming a Christian (including repentance, confession, water baptism, forgiveness)."[73]

The event of becoming a Christian does not always conform to a set pattern or order. The following events are often associated with the experience of Christian conversion in Acts.

A presentation of the gospel

In every example where persons become a Christian they encounter the story of Jesus. Before conversion, people hear the gospel, the story of the life, death, and resurrection of Jesus. The effect of this story upon those who listen led Paul to conclude that this gospel is God's power for salvation (Rom. 1:16). The gospel fosters faith in Jesus.

A response of faith

In response to hearing the gospel people either turn away or toward Jesus. They either have a beginning faith in Jesus and his word or they refuse to listen. For those who turn toward Jesus a typical response is, "What must I do to be saved?" (Acts 16:30, 2:37) One answer that became a common response was, "Believe on the Lord Jesus and you will be saved" (Acts 16:3). Paul's summary statement reads, "If you confess with your lips that Jesus is Lord and believe in your heart that God raised him from the dead, you will be saved" (Rom. 10:9). This simple explanation of the way of salvation describes the heart of Christian conversion in terms of what is asked of us.

An invitation to baptism

In every example of initiation/conversion in Acts, those who respond in faith to the gospel are invited to be baptized in water (e.g. Acts 8:36f). Jesus is the model.

The gift of the Holy Spirit

Peter's conclusion is that Christian initiation involved receiving the gift of the Holy Spirit (Acts 2:38). Whether the gift of the Spirit precedes baptism (Acts 10:45-48, 2:1- 4),follows baptism (Acts 8:12-17, 19:1-6), or occurs at the same time as water baptism (Acts 2:30-41), the gift of the Holy Spirit is an essential part of the initiation/conversion experience. This points again to the baptism of Jesus as the basic model for Christian baptism. In the Anabaptist tradition the confirmation of the Spirit and water baptism are part of the same event.[74]

Christian community and service

The new Christian became part of the Christian community (Acts 2:42ff). Here they would be trained to be disciples of Jesus. In this family they would grow up and grow together in Christ. The goal was love, holiness of life, obedience to Christ, service, and life together.

3. Baptism as a Sign that in Christ we have died to sin and have been raised up by the power of God to live a new life

Paul begins with the premise that the Christian is "in Christ." Jesus' image of the vine and the branches conveys this same unity. We are "baptized into (Christ's) death" (Rom. 6:3), "buried with him in baptism" (Col. 2:12a), "raised with him through faith in the power of God" (Col. 2:12b). We are included and identified in the death, burial and resurrection of Jesus Christ. Our baptism is a two-fold sign that in Christ we have died to sin and been made alive to the life of God (Rom. 6:11). The point of our identifi- cation with Christ in our baptism is that it shows that we are free from sin and free to serve God. What happened to Christ has happened to us. Rather than being an excuse to sin or live an immoral life our baptism is God's declaration of our separation from the powers of evil. Our baptism is God's declaration of our resurrection to a new life.

Paul's conversion experience shapes his theology. The experience of meeting Jesus, his repentance, healing, the event of his baptism in water and Spirit all mark a transformational moment in his life. Everything is changed. His experience of initiation/conversion represents a new beginning, a crossing over from an old way of thinking and living to a new way. Paul's conversion experience is like Israel's experience crossing through the water of the Red Sea or the Jordan River.

Paul's baptism represents a sign that he has in Christ left behind his old life and crossed over into life in the promised land. It represents a reminder that he is finished with sin. From now on the Holy Spirit is alive in Paul to kill whatever evil remains. For Paul baptism is a symbol that he is in Christ, that in Christ he has died to sin and has become part of a new creation.

As we go down into the water the old life is drowned. We leave behind the old ways, our sins are forgiven, we let go of our self, we die, we are crucified with Christ, we yield ourselves to God. And as we are lifted up out of the water we are being raised up by the power of God to live a new life. Our baptism here symbolizes the beginning of a whole new world. If Christ is risen then the end of the old creation has occurred. If Christ is risen then the new age has begun. This is why Easter has become the most common time to baptize new believers.

4. Baptism as a Sign that in Christ we are united to one another.

> As many of you as were baptized into Christ have clothed
> yourselves with Christ. There is no longer Jew or Greek, there
> is no longer slave or free, there is no longer male and female;
> for all of you are one in Christ Jesus" (Gal.3:27-28).

Our baptism into Christ is as if we have clothed ourselves with
Christ. Ethnic identity is often identified by clothing. In our baptism in
Christ we take off our ethnic clothing, our fancy pants, our professional
hats, our distinguishing tassels, our jewels and medals. We take off the
clothes that mark our national identity, gender, class and color. We put
on the plain and holy clothes of Christ.

Not only are we united to Christ in baptism, we are in Christ
united to one another. We become one family, one people in Christ.
"For in the one Spirit we are all baptized into one body -Jews or Greeks,
slaves or free - and we were all made to drink of one Spirit" (1 Cor.
12:13). The effect of coming to know Christ is that Christ creates a bond
of peace (Eph. 4:3-5). Our loyalty undergoes a shift from race, class,
family, and nation to Christ. We are separated from the world and
gathered into the community of Jesus. Christian baptism represents our
marriage to Christ and the Church. In the service of baptism this is
symbolized by the kiss of peace, the right hand of fellowship, and the
welcoming embrace of the community.

5. Baptism as a Vow of Obedience

> ...and this water (the flood) symbolizes baptism that now saves
> you also - not the removal of dirt from the body but the pledge
> of a good conscience toward God. It saves you by the
> resurrection of Jesus Christ, who has gone into heaven and is
> at God's right hand - with angels, authorities and powers in
> submission to him (1 Pet. 3:21-22 NIV).

Peter may here be using baptism to represent the whole process
by which people become Christians.[75] The water of baptism saves not
by itself but by the power of the resurrection of Christ who has
disarmed the authorities and powers that have oppressed and enslaved
us. The waters of baptism, of the flood, and of the Jordan are signs of
salvation and the deliverance of God from the powers of death, slavery,
and the desert.

Peter's focus is here on baptism as dedication. The resurrection
of Jesus saves us; for our part we pledge obedience to Christ. God sets
us free from sin and we give to God our pledge to break with sin.
Baptism is a sign of our discipleship and commitment to Christ.

Baptism is a vow of obedience to Christ, a believer's decision to follow Christ in life. This understanding of baptism is also evident in 1 Corinthians 10:1-13. Paul's argument is that just because Israel was "baptized into Moses...into the sea" it did not keep them from being "struck down in the desert." Baptism cannot be used as an excuse to sin or lead an immoral life. Rather baptism is a pledge of our allegiance to Christ.

An Anabaptist understanding of Christian baptism identifies baptism with what Kenneth Davis calls "monastic initiation vows."[76] Paul Lederach writes, "Baptism is the means through which the reborn believer commits himself or herself to a life of obedience in fellowship with other believers and is enrolled in the visible community of salvation."[77]

A summary of the various images of baptism in the New Testament is provided in *Baptism, Eucharist and Ministry*.

> Baptism is participation in Christ's death and resurrection (Rom. 6:3-5; Col. 2:12); a washing away of sin (1 Cor. 6:11); a new birth (John 3:5); an enlightenment by Christ (Eph.5:14); a reclothing in Christ (Gal. 3:27); a renewal by the Spirit (Titus 3:5); the experience of salvation by the flood (1 Pet. 3:20-21); an exodus from bondage (1 Cor. 10:1-2); and a liberation into a new humanity in which barriers of division...are transcended (Gal. 3:27-28); 1 Cor. 12:13) The images are many, but the reality is one.[78]

B. Three Services of Baptism

What follows is a description of three services of baptism: 1) a third century service of baptism as described by Hippolitus in his book, The Apostolic Tradition;[79] 2) the Celebration of the Sacrament of Initiation, the recent Catholic rite of baptism as described in the RCIA;[80] and 3) the baptism service used by the Foundation Mennonite Church.

1. The Apostolic Tradition

Preparation of the candidates before Easter
Immersion of the naked candidates in water
A final renunciation of Satan
The sealing of the Spirit
The kiss of peace and Eucharist

2. The Celebration of the Sacraments of Initiation - RCIA

On Holy Saturday before Easter the day is spent in preparation. There is a time for reflection and prayer, recitation of the Creed, the Ephphatha rite, a prayer for God to open the ears and mouth to hear and to share the gospel. One chooses a Christian name followed by a prayer of blessing. The following service occurs on Easter Sunday.

Service of Light
Liturgy of the Word
Celebration of Baptism
    Presentation of the candidates
    A litany of prayer remembering the saints
    Prayer of blessing the water
    A profession of faith involving renunciation of sin and a
        profession of faith in God
Baptism
Explanatory rites
    Anointing after baptism
    Clothing with a baptismal garment
    Presentation with a lighted candle
Celebration of Confirmation
    Invitation
    Laying on of hands
    Anointing with chrism, sealing with the Holy Spirit
Renewal of Baptismal Promises
    Renunciation of sin
    Profession of faith
    Sprinkling with baptismal water
Liturgy of the Eucharist

3. Foundation Mennonite Service of Baptism[81]

Gathering to Worship

Prelude and Welcome

In the name of Jesus Christ we welcome you. It is good that you have come. We have been gathered by the Spirit of God on this special occasion to witness and to share in this celebration of Christian baptism.

For those who have been baptized into Christ and the Church, may this service of baptism be an occasion for you to reaffirm your vows of baptism. May this event serve to confirm and enhance the meaning and significance of your own baptism. May your devotion to Christ and your commitment to serve Christ be deepened.

And for those who may not have been baptized into Christ and the Church we hope that this service of baptism may witness to your mind and heart of the good news of Jesus Christ. May God use this occasion to bless your life, may your ears be open to hear the gospel of Jesus. We begin with the words of Jesus as recorded by the Apostle Matthew.

The Commission of Jesus in Matthew 28:16-20.

The word of Jesus establishes the practice of Christian baptism. It is his command that we make disciples of all nations, that we baptize and teach people to obey Jesus Christ as Lord. In accordance with these declarations of the Word of God, these candidates have presented themselves before us for the purpose of being baptized.

Prayer of Blessing

> O God, our creator and the creator of the world,
>> Be present at this baptism, as a symbol of re-creation. You
>> love all you have made and desire their salvation.
> By your Spirit you have drawn these people to Christ.
> In baptism seal your mercy's work in their lives.
> Let it lead them to the secret of the cross:
>> to be crucified with Christ
>> so Christ may rise to life in them.
> Bring them into the companionship of your church.
> Set them on the narrow way.
> Draw them deeper into your love.
> Give them the joy of their salvation,
>> for the sake of your Son, our Savior. AMEN[82]

Celebration and Praise

Reading of Psalm 100
Songs: Holy, Holy, Holy (*Hymnal, A Worship Book*, 5); Be exalted O Lord; Majesty; and Shine, Jesus Shine.

Ministry of the Word

> (Readers will recite the four passages listed below. After each reading the meaning of the Word will be proclaimed. Following the proclamation of the Word, the symbolic action chosen to make the meaning of the Word visible and effective will be described.)

Mark 1:9-11

The baptism of Jesus defines the meaning of Christian baptism. As Jesus is raised up out of the water, the heavens are torn open, the Holy Spirit comes upon him, and he hears a voice from heaven speaking words of love. So also in Christian baptism the heavens are opened and we receive the gift of the Holy Spirit who was already at work in our new birth. And we pray that each person being baptized will hear God's word of love.

The symbol that is a sign of the gift of the Spirit is the laying on of hands and the prayer "May the heavens be opened and may you receive the gift of the Spirit."

Romans 6:3-10

Baptism is a sign that in Christ we have died to sin and that in Christ we have been raised up by the power of God to live a new life. It represents the end of our old way of living and the beginning of a new life.

As we go down into the water the old life is drowned. We are dying to self. As we are being lifted up out of the water we are being raised up by the power of God to live a new life. We know our sins are forgiven, that we are clean.

Galatians 3:27-28

Baptism is also a sign that in Christ we are united to one another. In Christ we are one family, we become part of the Christian community. We take off our old clothes, our professional tassels, our hats, our fancy pants, our jewels and medals and we put on the plain clothes of Christ. The Spirit of God draws us into the body of Christ, creating bonds of love and peace. These bonds of peace and love are symbolized by the kiss of peace, the welcoming embrace of the community, and our commitment to the rule of Christ.

1 Peter 3:21-22 (NIV)

Peter says that we are saved in our baptism by the resurrection of Jesus Christ. God gives us salvation and we give to God the pledge of our allegiance. Baptism is our vow of obedience to Christ. Baptism is a sign of our choice to be a disciple of Jesus, to follow and serve Jesus in life. The vows that follow are verbal signs of our willingness to love and live in obedience to Jesus Christ.

Two other symbols that appear in this service are the lighted candle and the white robes. The lighted candle is a symbol to us that the light of Christ has come into the world, into our lives, and that from now on we are called together to be the light of Christ in the world. The white robes are a sign that in Christian baptism we take off the clothes of sin and put on the clothes of Christ. We are robed in the righteousness and holiness of God.

Confessions of Faith

A. Personal Witness.

We invite each mentor to present for baptism their companion. (The mentor interview provides the mentors a way of helping their companion prepare this testimony. Following the mentors'presentation the pastor says to each companion:)

Companion (name), will you give witness to your faith in Jesus Christ?

B. Confession of the Apostles' Creed.

Leader: Do you believe in one true, eternal and almighty God, who is Creator and Preserver of all things visible and invisible?
Seeker: I believe.
Leader: Do you believe in Jesus Christ as the only begotten Son of God; that he is the only Savior of humankind; that he lived and taught among us; that he died upon the cross, and gave himself a sacrifice for our sins; and he arose again that through him we might have eternal life?
Seeker: I believe.
Leader: Do you believe in the Holy Spirit, who proceeds from the Father and the Son, who comforts us, makes us a holy people, and guides us into all truth?
Seeker: I believe.

C. A Renunciation of Satan and the Realm of Evil

Leader: Jesus is Lord. The power of Satan, of sin, death, and evil is strong, but the power of God shown to us in the resurrection of Jesus Christ is stronger. Jesus Christ was revealed for the purpose of destroying the works of the devil (1 Jn 3:8). In the life, death and resurrection of Jesus Christ, God has disarmed the powers of evil and triumphed over them (Col. 2:15). Because of the victory of Jesus Christ we will fear no evil (Ps. 23:4).
Leader: Do you, in the power of Christ renounce Satan and all the works of darkness and your own selfish will and sinful desires?
Seeker: I do.

Congregational Song: I am the bread of life
                        (*Hymnal, A Worship Book*, 472)

Covenants of Commitment

A. The rule of Christ

Leader: Your baptism is a sign that you are joined to Christ and his
         church. Do you desire upon this confession of faith and
         baptism by water and the Spirit to be received into the church
         of Jesus Christ; and are you willing to give and receive counsel
         and live in fellowship with other believers and to participate
         in the mission of God for the world?
Seeker: I am.

B. A renewal of baptismal vows by the congregation

As we now receive you into the fellowship of the church, we make this
covenant with you as we renew our own covenant with God:
          to bear each others' burdens,
          to assist in times of need;
          to share our gifts and possessions,
          to forgive as Christ has forgiven us,
          to support each other in joy and sorrow,
          and in all things to work for the common good,
          thus making known Christ's presence among us to the glory of
          God.
As we unite with each other now, may we all be joined with Christ, our
          Lord. (*Hymnal, A Worship Book*, 777.)

Congregational Hymn: The Servant Song, (*Hymnal, A Worship Book*, 307)

Offering and Offertory

Baptism and the Gift of the Holy Spirit

        (Candidate and mentor walk together into the water of
baptism. The minister and the mentor lay on hands.)

Leader: Upon the confession of your faith made before God and these
         witnesses, we baptize you in the name of the Father and of the
         Son and of the Holy Spirit. May the heavens be opened and
         may you receive the gift of the Holy Spirit.

Ministry of Love and Fellowship

Welcome (The mentors and their companions walk together to the edge
of the water. Each candidate is greeted there by an elder of the
community who extends the hand of fellowship saying):

In the name of Christ and the church I give you my hand and
bid you arise. Just as Christ was raised from the dead by the
glory of God so you too shall walk in the power of the
resurrection. Remain in Christ and Christ will remain in you.
Christ has chosen you to go and bear fruit.

The Kiss of Peace

Presentation with a Lighted Candle

Christ is in you and you are the light of the world. Let your
light shine before others, so that they may see your good
works and give glory to your Father in heaven.

Congregational Song: The light of Christ

Benediction

CHAPTER IV

A PRACTICAL GUIDE TO MENTORING IN THE CONGREGATION

On Calling Forth Mentors and Disciples

In our congregation our best attempts to reach non-Christians did not result in anyone becoming interested in pursuing baptism. We did have four youth within the congregation between the ages of eight and fourteen who expressed a desire for baptism. There were also four adults who had within the year either become Christians or renewed their commitment to Christ. These eight people were invited to be involved in a three month process of Christian formation. We briefly described the mentoring process, the four services of initiation, and the goal of baptism. To simplify matters the discipling process was the same for the youth as for the adults. Attention was given to communicating ideas and experiences in as simple a manner as possible.

Having eight companions we needed eight mentors who would be willing to give themselves to the work of making disciples. For this project mentors were chosen on the basis of availability.

People who are willing to consider being a spiritual mentor are given the chapter on Discipleship and Mentoring to read. They are invited to meet together and share about the work of mentoring. They are also introduced to the Companion Interview as a tool for mentoring. Emphasis is placed on the idea that we learn best from the practice of mentoring. It may be helpful to provide the prospective mentors with a list of those images of mentoring that the church may wish to stress.

In pairing mentors and companions we prayed for wisdom and did the best we could to provide each companion with an appropriate mentor. We chose to provide men with male mentors and women with female mentors. I approached the mentors and asked them if they would be willing to be a mentor to a specific companion we had selected. If they responded positively we then asked the companions if they would affirm the selected mentor.

The Period and Service of Welcome

A. The Mentor Relationship

1. The mentor is responsible to arrange for a time to meet together before the service of welcome. Plan to meet for one or two hours. The mentor should read Chapter three of this project.

2. Pray together in silence to begin. Share together about parents, occupations, interests, church affiliations, marriage status, families. After about twenty minutes the mentor might say, "Share with me the story of your spiritual journey." Listen for about twenty minutes.

3. Introduce the Companion Interview. The mentor may say:

> I have been given a tool called a Companion Interview. This is a series of questions patterned after questions and statements attributed to Jesus by the writer of the gospel of Mark. I will ask you a question and listen to your response. There are no right or wrong answers, only your answers. Of course, you may decline to answer any question or ask for clarifications. I assure you that our conversation will be confidential.

4. Go through the Companion Interview for the period of welcome. Feel free to omit questions you may not be comfortable asking. At the end of the meeting arrange to meet again before the service of welcome. Encourage your companion to begin reading the gospel of Mark and commit yourselves to pray for each other daily.

5. Begin the second meeting in silent prayer. One purpose of this meeting is to help prepare your companions for the service of welcome. Share with your companions that during this service they will be asked to respond to the following questions, "What do you ask of God's church?" and "What do you ask of God?" Listen to their responses and help them to discern their own answers. A simple response is best, one word or a phrase.

6. Prepare your companions for the service by assuring them that you will be with them. Encourage them to relax and to listen during the service. It is not necessary to read through the service with them beforehand. Pray together and share your commitment to pray for them during the week. Is there something they would like you to pray for? Would they be willing to pray for you?

7. Prepare a prayer that you will pray for your companions during the service of welcome.

8. Meet with your companion during the week following the service of welcome. Share about their experience of welcome, the songs, the scriptures, the prayers, the service, the people. Pray together and share what you are reading in the gospel of Mark. Continue your disciplines of praying for each other during the coming week.

B. Companion Interview for the Period of Welcome

1. Do you read the Bible? What is one of your favorite Bible stories?

2. Jesus said, "I have come to call not the righteous, but sinners" (Mark 2:17). What does this mean to you?

3. Jesus said, "No one puts new wine into old wineskins; otherwise, the wine will burst the skins, and the wine is lost, and so are the skins; but one puts new wine into fresh wineskins" (Mark 2:22). "The Sabbath was made for humankind, and not humankind for the Sabbath; so the Son of Man is Lord even of the Sabbath" (Mark 2:27,28). What do you think of Sunday church?

What is your worst experience of church or religion? What is your best experience?

4. In the Parable of the Sower in Mark 4:1-20 what kind of soil best describes you?

5. Jesus was speaking to a crowd. His family came to bring him home. The people told Jesus that his family was waiting for him. Jesus replied, "Who are my mother and my brothers?...Whoever does the will of God is my brother and sister" (Mark 3:35).

When you think about your mother and father what stands out? Was she/he a religious person?

What persons have been most influential in your religious experience? Did they pray; do good; read the Bible; attend church; live a moral life?

Was God a part of your life as a child?

6. Jesus and the disciples were together in a boat. "A great windstorm arose, and the waves beat into the boat, so that the boat was already being swamped. But (Jesus) was in the stern, asleep on the cushion; and they woke him up and said to him, "Teacher, do you not care that we are perishing?" He woke up and rebuked the wind and said to the sea, "Peace! Be still!" Then the wind ceased, and there was a dead calm. He said to them, "Why are you afraid? Have you still no faith?" (Mark 4:37-40)

Are you at peace? Are you at peace with God?

Do you have faith?

7. On a high mountain Jesus was "transfigured" before Peter, James, and John. Out of a cloud came a voice saying, "This is my beloved Son; listen to him!" (Mark 9:7)

Has there been any moment of great wonder, awe, or joy that has shaped your life, any significant experience in worship, in nature, in the arts, a dream or a vision?

How do you listen to Jesus?

8. Bartimaeus was a blind beggar who kept shouting for Jesus to have mercy on him. Jesus, giving the blind man his attention, asked him, "What do you want me to do for you?" (Mark 10:51)

What would you want Jesus to do for you?

9. Jesus said, "You shall love the Lord your God with all your heart and with all your soul, and with all your mind, and with all your strength...You shall love your neighbor as yourself" (Mark 12:30,31a).

Do you love God? How is this love expressed?

Tell me about a time when you felt closest to God, a time when you were most aware of God's love?

10. What are your dreams? What are your faith goals?

The Period of Decision

A. The Mentor Relationship

1. The sponsors will meet with their companions at least once prior to the service of decision. This service will provide the companions opportunity to publicly confess Jesus as their Lord and Savior. The service will give occasion for the mentors to give testimony to their companions' faith in Christ.

2. The following questions for discernment may be appropriate for this purpose: Is there evidence of a beginning faith in Christ? Have they begun to become acquainted with Jesus and his teaching? Are they turning toward Jesus or away from Jesus? Are they willing to identify themselves with Jesus and his church? Will they confess Jesus as their Lord and Savior? Are they aware of the cost of following Jesus? As their sponsor can I give testimony to their beginning faith in Jesus Christ?

B. Companion Interview for the Period of Decision

1. Jesus came proclaiming the good news of God, saying, "The time is fulfilled, and the kingdom of God has come near; repent, and believe the good news" (Mark 1:15).

What do you think was the good news of God that Jesus proclaimed? Do you believe him?

2. Jesus said, "Follow me and I will make you fish for people." And immediately they left their nets and followed him (Mark 1:17,18).

What does it mean for you to follow Jesus? Is there anything that you may need to leave behind to follow Jesus?

3. Jesus said, "Son, your sins are forgiven" (Mark.2:5).

Do you know that your sins are forgiven?

4. Jesus told the scribes, "Those who are well have no need of a physician, but those who are sick; I have come to call not the righteous but sinners" (Mark 2:17). What is a "sinner"?

5. Jesus asked his disciples, "Who do you say that I am?" (Mark 8:29). How do you respond to this question?

6. Jesus called the crowd with his disciples, and said to them, "If any want to become my followers, let them deny themselves and take up their cross and follow me" (Mark 8:34). Are you willing to suffer for Jesus?

7. On a high mountain Jesus was "transfigured" before Peter, James, and John. Out of a cloud came a voice saying, "This is my beloved Son; listen to him!" (Mark 9:7). Are you willing to listen to Jesus?

8. There once was a rich man whom Jesus loved. Jesus told him to "sell what you own, and give the money to the poor, and come, follow me" (Mark 10:21). Would you be willing to follow Jesus if he asked you in love to sell what you own and give to the poor?

9. Three women brought spices to anoint Jesus who had died. When they came to the tomb they were greeted by a messenger who said to them, "He has been raised" (Mark 16:6). Do you believe Jesus is risen from the dead?

The Period of Purification and Enlightenment

A. The Mentor Relationship

1. Plan to meet together following the service of decision to share about that experience. How was God present to them in that meeting? Begin the time together in silent prayer. Be quiet together for five minutes and then share after this time of silence.

2. To prepare for this meeting the mentors should read from chapter three of this paper the section entitled, "The Period and Service of Purification and Enlightenment", familiarize themselves with the Service of Purification and Enlightenment from the same chapter and read through the Companion Interview for this period.

3. It may be appropriate during these weeks to schedule a day apart or a retreat weekend for a time of extended prayer, quietness, fasting, meditation and rest. This could be done with others from the congregation. It may become apparent that confession, forgiveness, healing need to occur. Do the best you can. Do not make any attempt to force confession. Perhaps the mentor and the companion would be led by God to make a complete moral inventory of their life and share this with another person. Hold each other accountable to the practice of those spiritual disciplines that you have decided to practice, especially the discipline of reading scripture and praying for each other. Remember to practice images of mentoring from chapter two; bless your companion, carry them to Jesus, listen, be their friend, love them, help them to see Jesus, pray for them, encourage "doing good."

B.   The Companion Interview for the Period of Purification and Enlightenment.

1. Jesus came proclaiming the good news of God, saying "The time is fulfilled, and the kingdom of God has come near; repent, and

believe the good news" (Mark 1:15). Are you aware of any change that God is working in your life?

2. Jesus rebuked an unclean spirit saying, "Be silent, and come out of him!" (Mark.1:25). Is there anything in your life you would ask Jesus to remove?

3. After Jesus was baptized, the Spirit immediately drove him out into the wilderness. He was in the wilderness forty days, tempted by Satan; and he was with the wild beasts; and the angels waited on him (Mark 1:12,13a). Is there any besetting sin that keeps reoccurring? How do you respond to temptation?

4. Jesus said, "Son, your sins are forgiven" (Mark 2:5). Do you know your sins are forgiven?

5. A child had died. Jesus went to where she was. He took her by the hand and said to her, "Talitha cum," which means, "Little girl, get up!" (Mk.5:41). Is there anything in your life that you would want Jesus to awaken?

6. The disciples were hungry and tired. Jesus said to them, "Come away to a deserted place all by yourselves and rest awhile" (Mark 6:31). What are you hungry for? Are you able to rest in the presence of God?

7. They brought to him a deaf man who had an impediment in his speech; and they begged him to lay his hand on him. He took him aside in private, away from the crowd, and put his fingers into his ears, and spat and touched his tongue. Then looking up to heaven, he sighed and said to him, "Ephphatha," that is, "Be opened." And immediately his ears were opened, his tongue released, and he spoke plainly" (Mark 7:32-35). Is there any obstacle or impediment that you are aware of that God needs to open up for you?

8. In the ninth chapter of Mark Jesus twice asks his disciples, "What are you arguing about?" (Mark 9:16,33). What do you argue about? Do you ever want to be "the greatest?"

9. Jesus said, "If any of you put a stumbling block before one of these little ones who believe in me, it would be better for you if a great millstone were hung around your neck and you were thrown into the sea. If your hand causes you to stumble, cut it off" (Mark 9:42,43a). Has anyone ever harmed you as a child? Is there anything that needs to be cut out of your life?"

10. Jesus said, "So I tell you, whatever you ask for in prayer, believe that you have received it, and it will be yours. Whenever you stand praying, forgive, if you have anything against anyone; so that your Father in heaven may also forgive you your trespasses" (Mark 11:24,25). What is something you would ask for in prayer? Is there anyone you need to forgive?

11. Jesus prayed, "not what I want, but what you want" Mark 14:36). Are you willing to yield your self to do the will of God rather than insisting on your own way?

12. Jesus cried out, "My God, my God, why have you forsaken me?" (Mark 15:34). Have you ever felt forsaken by God?

Preparation for Baptism

A. The Mentor Relationship

1. The mentor is to read from chapter three of this paper the section entitled "The Period and Service of Baptism" and become acquainted with the Companion Interview for this period. Schedule a meeting with your companion. Begin with silent prayer. Share together about your experience of the Service of Purity and Light. Read the Companion Interview for the Service of Baptism.
2. Following the service of baptism arrange to meet together. Share together about your experience of the service. How was God present to you in this meeting?
3. This may be your final meeting. You have served to introduce your companions to Christ and the church; they have begun the process of discipling. This is only the beginning. We have done our best to make it a good beginning. There will hopefully be other mentors that God will provide our companions and ourselves as we continue our journey to become like Jesus.

B. The Companion Interview for the Service of Baptism

The sponsors are to help their companions to think about and write down their personal witness to Jesus Christ. By reading together the following scriptures and listening to their responses a simple word of witness will hopefully emerge. This testimony is an opportunity for the companions to be a Christian witness to their friends. The length of this time of witness may be as brief as a few sentences, or as long as a few minutes. Sponsors do not tell their companions what to say. They are to listen to them and help them to discern what word God would have them share.
1. At that time Jesus came from Nazareth in Galilee and was baptized by John in the Jordan. As Jesus was coming up out of the water, he saw heaven being torn open and the Spirit descending on him like a dove. And a voice came from heaven: "You are my Son whom I love; with you I am well pleased" (Mark 1:9-11 NIV).

Have you experienced the Holy Spirit in your life? It is our prayer that you would hear in your baptism God's word of love addressed that "you are my daughter/son whom I love."
2. And Jesus came to them and said to them, "All authority in heaven and on earth has been given to me. Go therefore and make disciples of all nations, baptizing them in the name of the Father and of

the Son and of the Holy Spirit, teaching them to obey everything that I have commanded you. And remember, I am with you always, to the end of the age" (Matthew 28:18-20).

Is it your choice to be a disciple of Jesus, to be baptized, and to live in obedience to Him?

3. Jesus said to him, "Go home to your friends, and tell them how much the Lord has done for you, and what mercy he has shown you" (Mark 5:19).

Speaking to your friends at your baptism, what do you want them to know that the Lord has done for you?   How have you experienced God's mercy?

4. During the service of baptism the sponsors will present their companions to the congregation by name and share briefly what word God gives them to share. For example:"

It is my honor to present (name) to Christ and the Church for baptism. I bear witness to (name) faith in Jesus Christ. I pray that (name) would know the hope to which God has called her/him."

5. Sponsors are to go through the service of baptism with their companions. Perhaps they have some questions. Go over the different symbols that will be used during the service of baptism. Share together about what these symbols mean to you. Encourage companions to listen, to enjoy, and to give their attention to the presence of God in the service of baptism. Sponsors should pray with their companions.

6. Some metaphors of baptism and salvation that may be helpful in preparing a testimony:

Baptism is a sign to me that the Holy Spirit has come into my life.

Becoming a Christian was like becoming part of a new family.

Jesus Christ is like a foundation upon which I want to build my life.

Baptism is like a marriage ceremony in which I am publicly announcing my decision to have a lifetime relationship with Jesus Christ and his people.

Baptism is like an ordination service saying that I am prepared to serve Jesus.

Accepting Jesus Christ as my Lord and Savior was like receiving a gift.

Other (write your own!)

7. The mentors may wish to purchase a gift to give to their companions following the service of baptism.

CHAPTER V

CONCLUSION AND EVALUATION

The focus of this project has been to develop a discipline that integrates the experience of congregational worship, the accountability of a mentor relationship, and the practice of spiritual disciplines as means to the end of growth in Christ. The following observations are drawn from my experience of implementing this project and from the congregational evaluation of the project which is given in Appendix I.

On the Service of Initiation

The four services of initiation: Welcome, Decision, Purification and Baptism were intended to be evangelistic. They were designed to proclaim the gospel and invite a response of faith. However, responses to the question on evangelism in the evaluation indicated some reservations about the evangelistic impact of the service.

I think we tend to identify evangelism with a revival service. In that sense, these services were not as specific in eliciting a conversion experience in relationship to the preaching of the Word. With some imagination and creativity the services of Welcome and Decision could be presented as a version of the old-time revival service.

The kind of church growth envisioned in this paper is church growth through discipleship. Our priority is to make disciples through the means of spiritual friendship, spiritual disciplines, congregational worship, and mission. Evangelism, peace, justice, worship, service submit to the rule of discipleship. Evangelism and peace are spiritual disciplines that serve the master plan of discipliship. The first work of the church is to make discipes who make love and peace. Life in Christ is the priority. Church growth that is not the result of discipleship will not endure. Church growth is not the goal, discipleship is the goal.

These services of initiation presented in this project may be most appropriate for a middle-class, smaller, white, non-ethnic, educated and urban congregation. I see no reason why they cannot be adapted to other settings.

The sharing of stories by candidates and mentors in the Service of Welcome was appreciated. Although most were afraid of public speaking, with help and encouragement this fear gave way to a willingness to share.

The age for baptism was not a significant issue for the congregation. This discipling process of congregational worship and mentoring would seem to work best with people ages 12 and up. The companion interview had to be simplified for the younger companions.

The Service of Welcome is not to be confused with welcoming visitors. It is designed to welcome companions to a process of discipleship. There must be a beginning faith, a beginning interest in Christ and the church. We are welcoming serious seekers of Christ - people who are willing to begin a process of discipling. The gospel has already been proclaimed and they have been invited to follow Christ.

On Baptism

Why should we wait months to baptize a person who makes a confession of faith in Christ, especially when the New Testament demonstrates that it was the church's practice to baptize upon confession of faith (See Acts 2:38f; 8:37; 9:10; 22:16)? In the words of the Ethiopian eunuch, "What is to prevent me from being baptized?" (Acts 8:37). The process of discipling we have proposed would seem to ask the eunuch to wait three or four months. Waiting for baptism for an extended period of time after conversion of faith in Christ cuts across some evangelical Christian practice. By thinking about conversion as both an event and a process are we denying people the grace of the Holy Spirit by prolonging their baptism? Why should we balk at Philip's "slam-dunk" baptism of the eunuch?

Within 150 years the Early Church had developed a structured process for preparing candidates for baptism. Each candidate was given a sponsor and entered into a three- year apprenticeship designed to prepare them for living as Christians in the church and in the world. Their baptism was delayed up to three years. Did this change occur because of Christianity's encounter with a pagan society? A pagan cultural setting presented the need for a different approach to preparation for baptism than did a Jewish cultural setting.

In Philip's case, he did act as the eunuch's mentor. He explains the Scripture and tells the eunuch the good news about Jesus. (v.3) Both of them are traveling. There is no reason to delay his baptism. Nothing occurs to Philip that would prevent it. Philip would have responded differently if the Ethiopian was not a seeker of God. If the eunuch had been to Jerusalem not to worship God but were on his way to war, Philip would have waited before he baptized.

Our structures must not impede the direction of the Holy Spirit. We want to do what is best, to baptize and disciple people so that they would believe and be faithful to Christ. If the best is to baptize quickly, then we should. This is a valid option. It is also a valid option to wait. We should not be in a hurry or cause unnecessary delay. People may get married or baptized in a hurry; yet it is often best to take our time, prepare, share, and celebrate these events together as a community.

One's theological perspective affects how much one can enthusiastically affirm this kind of discipling process. This project viewed conversion as both an event and a process. People who find this balance unacceptable may be less affirming of the process. Those who view conversion primarily as a process may object to having people make hard choices and early commitments, whereas those who see conversion primarily as an event may not be as tolerant of process and development in this model of baptism. Those who see the baptism of the Spirit occurring at a second stage following water baptism may be uncomfortable with affirming that the baptism of Jesus is the prototype of baptism. In their experience, the baptism of the Holy Spirit has occurred at a time subsequent to their water baptism.

"When does the Spirit come upon us?" While I sympathize with those whose experience of the Spirit was subsequent to their water baptism, we cannot omit the words "be baptized with the Holy Spirit" from the Service of Baptism. Omit the Holy Spirit and there is no reason for baptism.

A related question has to do with viewing the Service of Decision as a sign to mark the companion's conversion experience. While I recognize that we cannot time conversion, that there are different conversions—to Christ, to the church, to peace, to simplicity—yet it is important that we give public witness to our conversion to Christ at a moment in time. Although this service may not reflect the precise moment of conversion, this is no reason to omit the testimony but is all the more reason to ask that the candidate decide to say yes or no to Christ. As a parent, a friend, or as the person being baptized, I do not need to date my conversion at this ceremony. I am free to say I became a Christian at some other time. We are calling pagans out of the world and into the Kingdom of God. There needs to be a time when this change is identified, celebrated and publicly affirmed. The wedding ceremony may not serve to mark the exact moment of love and commitment, yet we do not denigrate wedding ceremonies but value them as a sign to convey a previous and hopefully abiding love.

On Symbols, Rites, and Ceremonies

In this project, I have sought to appreciate the use of symbols and rites in worship. A symbol is a visible sign of an invisible belief. External actions make visible internal meanings. Symbols and rituals are artistic ways of providing the community with a vision of God. They help to clarify values, create positive change, inspire beauty, and provide meaning. Symbols are meaningful to children and adults, they inspire the imagination and speak to the heart.

Whereas many in the congregation enjoyed the use of symbols in the services, some were cautious and a few did not value the use of symbols. I would make the following observations and refinements in this delicate matter.

In the future, I would avoid the use or language such as "rites and liturgy" and use the words "service or meeting." High Church language seemed to be offensive to a few i.. the congregation so I would change my vocabulary.

I would also simplify the prayers, readings, confessions and congregational responses in the various services. Often they were too wordy, too formal. I would be more committed to using the words of Scripture in the services and avoid borrowing too much vocabulary from other traditions.

The preaching of the Word must be central to the service. The Word of God can be read, prayed, confessed, but it must also be proclaimed. The sermon needs to provide direction and form to the service. Symbols, rites, and sacraments must be in balance with the Word.

The planned services must continue to be intentional but also adaptable; free to change and respond to positive criticism and evaluation. For example, in the Service of Decision I had the candidates for baptism sign their names in a book as a symbol of their names being written in the "Book of Life." Most people were uncomfortable with this action. There was confusion as to what the signing meant and some thought it rather presumptuous, that only God can sign our name into the book. In the future, we need to choose a more appropriate symbol to show our commitment to follow Christ. One suggestion was to have the candidate walk down the aisle, be greeted by their mentor, kneel and receive the blessing of Christ in the form of a prayer.

For some people the symbol of lighted candles at the baptism was unfamiliar. From the perspective of the candidates, these same candles were "beautiful," "fun," and "a sign to me that I am to be a light of Christ in the world." I would continue to encourage those who may not appreciate the use of symbols in worship to be open to learning to value this as an appropriate part of worship. People will learn to value symbols through practice.

In general men did not appreciate the symbols and signs as much as women. Men tended to focus more on the verbal content, some even seeing symbols as "intrusive," while women were more positive and responsive to the signs.

Ceremonies need to be better integrated into the normal congregational worship style. For this congregation, that means that we would maintain a "praise and worship" time, perhaps a time of sharing, and allow for "spontaneous" direction from the Holy Spirit. We do not want to be formal. We also need to be careful that these ceremonies do not focus exclusively on the needs of the candidate and ignore the needs of the congregation.

An unfortunate oversight occurred in the Service of Baptism. In two cases a parent assisted in the baptism of their children, while in another case, the parent wanted to assist but this desire was not communicated to the leadership. This option should have been more clearly identified. Good communication and preparation is essential if we are going to use worship as an occasion for discipleship.

The Mennonite Church needs to be willing to borrow and create symbols for use in worship. The Mennonite Church has let go of some old symbols such as plain clothes and the prayer covering that served to identify them as a unique people of Christ. The symbols of the land, the farm, the quilt and the casserole are passing away. Old names, old ways, and old forms need to be replaced by new symbols that will be meaningful for the future. How can we make visible the invisible presence of Christ in the meeting, in the Lord's Supper, in the prayers, and in the fellowship of the people? The symbol of the towel and basin could be more prominent. Symbols of mutual aid, peacemaking, community and simplicity could be utilized. We should not be too proud to borrow from other traditions. Lionel Trilling once said, "Immature artists imitate. Mature artists steal." Symbols are free to be borrowed just like "Bea Ekblad's" chocolate cake recipe.

A ritual is an external action with an internal meaning. Ritualism occurs when we lose the internal meaning, when we cherish the form but lose the meaning. We need to be wary of ritualism. The way to do this is not to avoid symbols but to choose symbols that lead us to Christ.

We need to develop other services with symbolic actions that speak to the Lord's Supper, footwashing, spiritual retreats, healing services, the blessing of children, and vocational discernment. This could be part of a revised minister's manual for the Mennonite Church.

On Mentoring

One fine result of the mentor relationship was that friendships were established. Mentors and companions affirmed the value of their time together. The mentoring relationship opened the discipling process up to the congregation. Discipleship was not just the responsibility of the pastor but a shared responsibility among the people.

Some felt that four months was too long to prepare for baptism but by far the majority of both mentors and companions felt it was not long enough. I believe this means that if the mentors were asked to do this again, they would attempt to meet more regularly with their companions and seek to be more faithful in this responsibility.

Mentors responded that they benefited as much as their companions from the time spent together. The Companion Interview from Mark was considered a useful tool but it should be refined and made available sooner than it was. The questions were not always appropriate.

One weakness was my failure to appropriately prepare the mentors. Written resource material must be available at the start of the mentoring process. And, in the future, I would consider meeting with the mentors to have them become more acquainted with the expectations of a mentor.

Although there are tests that are available concerning spiritual maturity, they were not administered. As to whether the companions, mentors, and congregation matured in Christ as the direct result of this project, I am unable to give a definitive answer. I was encouraged by the favorable response to this question on the congregation's evaluation.

The mentoring relationship was affirmed by the congregation as a valuable instrument for discipleship.

The method of discipleship is affected by the stage of spiritual development, the level of maturity, trust, the degree of commitment and love present in the community. Discipling in the congregation does not depend as much upon the perfect tool as it does upon a unity of fellowship in the Holy Spirit and a shared vision of discipling.

On Leadership

A central thesis of this paper has been that to grow in Christ we need to be discipled through a mentor relationship. We do not disciple ourselves. God disciples us through the gift of other Christians who are a means of divine grace. Spiritual disciplines require spiritual direction. Leadership must be committed to discipleship as a primary task. The more leadership is given to the work of discipleship the better the church will grow in Christ. Leadership must affirm the priority of discipleship. If the leadership does not desire to receive or to give spiritual care through mentoring it is unlikely that it will be an effective form of discipleship.

In regards to this project, experienced Christian leaders were willing to be mentors but were less willing to be mentored. All congregational leaders from the two congregations that participated in this project were willing to give spiritual care but only one actively sought to receive spiritual care through the mentoring process. Various factors may have contributed to this apparent reluctance of leaders to seek spiritual care through a mentoring relationship.

Leaders are busy and mentoring relationships demand a sacrifice of time. Whereas Christian leaders are willing to give their time for others they seem less open to make this sacrifice for their own self. A mentoring relationship in which leaders receive nurture can be perceived as a luxury for which we do not have time.

Leaders in a congregation may hesitate to commit themselves to a discipline of mentoring because the concept is not conceived as being collectively owned.   If the community is committed to collaborative and team ministry the chosen model of discipleship will need to emerge out of the collective will of the group. We may labor in vain unless the people sense an ownership in the project.

Leaders may be reluctant to seek spiritual care for themselves because it is not a felt need. Adequate spiritual nurture may already exist and mentoring is then seen as an unnecessary option. In this way of thinking it is the young Christian who needs a mentor while the experienced Christian needs to be rather than to seek a spiritual parent. It is perceived that mentoring a mature Christian is unnecessary because they are healthy enough.

Mentoring is at best a provisional guide to Christ, not a required discipline for all time. Yet I believe Christian leaders need to be open to a season of being mentored for a variety of reasons. For the healthy and mature Christian mentoring is a way to practice preventative spiritual care, of maintaining our relationship with God. The experience of being mentored is also an excellent way to learn the art of discipleship. We learn best through experience and practice. How can we hold another accountable unless we are being held accountable? How can we bless unless we are blessed? How can we hear confession unless we give confession? If we are called to GIVE spiritual care we must learn to RECEIVE spiritual care.

Though it may be true that there are times when mentoring is an unnecessary spiritual discipline for leaders, we need to be careful that this idea is not coming from a position of pride. We may be deceived by self-sufficiency and ego strength.

Christian leaders may hesitate to seek out spiritual care because it is unavailable or unacceptable. We should pray to God to provide us with the spiritual care we need.   Peer mentoring would be an excellent option for leaders.

Congregational leaders may be reluctant to seek spiritual care because they are timid, afraid of change, fearful of risk, or wary of spiritual intimacy.   The latter may be particularly true of male leadership.   Perhaps the reluctance of leaders to seek a mentoring relationship in this study was due to my reluctance to initiate it and to present mentoring as an option. In the future I would as a pastor in the congregation gently push the leadership of the church to pray for and seek a spiritual mentor. I would also clearly identify my own spiritual mentor and be open to the discernment of the church regarding this relationship.

A vision of congregational discipleship through worship, mentoring and spiritual disciplines represents a change in the way the religious system makes disciples. We are afraid of the spiritual intimacy that is implied in the concept.   In this sense this project has been

premature. *The congregation asked for friendship and I gave them a mentor.*
The order is first servant, friend then mentor. The expectation of
intimacy that is demanded in the mentor relationship requires a level of
trust that only service and friendship can build. In spiritual friendship,
friendship comes first. Love precedes intimacy.

Finally, there is a need for ritual leadership in the church, a
priestly function to leadership. The priesthood of believers affirms
priestly leadership within the congregation in regards to ritual. All are
called to praise God but not all are called to lead the congregation in
praise. All are priests, but not all are called to ritual leadership. Ritual
leadership should be valued. This demands our best effort, preparation
and prayer. In our congregation this kind of leadership will be shared
rather than the responsibility of one person.

A Final Observation

This project did not intentionally seek to involve companions in
the discipline of service, gift discernment, or small group fellowship. It
was my choice to limit the pre-baptismal stage to the process of
mentoring, spiritual disciplines and worship. The process should have
involved an educational agenda to teach facts, dogma, confession and
Mennonite belief. In the future I would seek to better integrate and
balance information with formation. It may be that gift discernment,
service, and small group fellowship is agenda for post-baptismal living.

As a carpenter I have found that the first time I do something
it takes me twice as long. I believe that if our congregation should
decide to use this form of discipleship again we will grow more familiar
with the process. We will mature and make necessary changes. The
first time through was difficult. Let us go on to make disciples, teaching
them to obey Jesus, that we may all grow together in Jesus Christ, to go
on to do the work God intends for us to do.

APPENDIX I

CONGREGATIONAL EVALUATION

Instruction: Circle one of the numbers following the statement. "5" means you strongly agree while "1" means you strongly disagree. Fill in the blanks and give comments as requested. [18 people responded to this evaluation, 7 mentors, 6 companions, and 5 persons from the congregation. The average response is listed in brackets.]

For Mentors

1. I was adequately prepared to be a spiritual mentor.

    1   2   3   4   5   [3.0]

2. I can positively affirm my experience of being a spiritual mentor.

    1   2   3   4   5   [4.2]

3. I would welcome the opportunity to be a spiritual mentor in the future.

    1   2   3   4   5   [4.4]

4. I believe the process of mentoring is an important tool to use in making disciples.

    1   2   3   4   5   [4.8]

5. What did I enjoy most about being a spiritual friend?

6. What would I change or do differently if I were to be a spiritual mentor again?

7. The Companion Interview from the gospel of Mark was a helpful tool.

    1   2   3   4   5   [4.0]

For Companions

1. I affirm my experience of being a spiritual companion.

    1   2   3   4   5   [4.6]

2. I believe I grew in Christ as a result of my initiation experience in worship and mentoring.

    1   2   3   4   5   [4.8]

3. I would recommend that other new Christians go through a similar process of Christian initiation and mentoring.

    1   2   3   4   5   [5.0]

4. What did I most enjoy about the mentoring experience?

5. What would I change?

6. The Companion Interview from the gospel of Mark was a helpful tool.

    1   2   3   4   5   [4.6]]

The Service of Welcome

1. The Service of Welcome was a good expression of Christian hospitality.

   1   2   3   4   5   [4.7]

2. The signing of the companions' senses was a meaningful experience.

   1   2   3   4   5   [4.2]

3. What would I change or do differently?

The Service of Decision

1. In the Service of Decision we became aware that we were chosen by God.

   1   2   3   4   5   [4.6]

2. I felt comfortable with the idea that this service would serve as a sign of the companion's decision to follow Christ.

   1   2   3   4   5   [4.0]

3. Conversion to Christ is both an event and a process.

   1   2   3   4   5   [4.8]

4. The candidates signing their names in the book was a meaningful experience to me.

   1   2   3   4   5   [4.3]

5. What would I change or do differently?

The Service of Enlightenment and Purification

1. It was appropriate to confess our sins, to ask God to remove any impediments from our lives.

    1   2   3   4   5   [4.8]

2. The prayers of exorcism and deliverance were acceptable.

    1   2   3   4   5   [4.2]

3. What would I change or do differently?

The Service of Baptism

1. The baptism of Jesus structures and orders Christian baptism.

    1   2   3   4   5   [4.6]

2. In baptism we affirm that the Holy Spirit is alive in the life of the person being baptized.

    1   2   3   4   5   [4.4]

3. Baptism is a sign that in Christ we have died to sin and have been raised by the power of God to live a new life.

    1   2   3   4   5   [5.0]

4. Baptism is a sign that in Christ we have been united to one another as sisters and brothers in God's family.

    1   2   3   4   5   [4.4]

5. Baptism is our vow of obedience to Jesus Christ.

    1   2   3   4   5   [4.5]

6. A person who was baptized as an infant may be rebaptized as an adult.

    1   2   3   4   5   [4.8]

7. Immersion is the preferred mode of baptism.

    1   2   3   4   5   [4.4]

8. The companion and mentor testimony was a meaningful experience.

    1   2   3   4   5   [4.8]

9. Children may be baptized at what age? [10]

10. What did the following symbols and actions mean to you?

    - immersion in water

    - confessions of faith

    - white robes

    - the greeting and kiss of peace

    - the lighted candles

11. What would I change or do differently?

General Questions

1. The various services of initiation were evangelistic.

    1   2   3   4   5   [4.0]

2. I would feel free to invite others to these services?

    1   2   3   4   5   [4.6]

3. I enjoyed the use of symbols in the services.

    1   2   3   4   5   [4.2]

4. I felt comfortable with the liturgical element in the worship services.

    1   2   3   4   5   [3.8]

5. This is a model of discipleship that I can affirm.

    1   2   3   4   5   [4.8]

6. The experience of worship and mentoring moved people toward Christ.

    1   2   3   4   5   [4.8]

7. The experience of worship and mentoring built friendship and mutual love.

    1   2   3   4   5   [4.8]

8. The experience of mentoring and worship enhanced our church's resolve to be of service to others.

    1   2   3   4   5   [3.8]

9. I would affirm the use of this form of discipleship in the future.

    1   2   3   4   5   [4.8]

NOTES

1.For a working paper on the congregational discipling model and vision see Mennonite Board of Congregational Ministries, P.O. Box 1245, Elkhart, IN 46515-1245.

2.Robert Kanigel, *Apprentice to Genius* (New York: Macmillan Pub., 1986).

3.Ibid., 60.

4.Ibid., 61.

5.Jonathan Cole, *Fair Science,* cited in Kanigel, 233.

6.Robert Merton, *Social Science* (New York: Macmillan, 1967).

7.Laurent Daloz, *Effective Teaching and Mentoring* (San Francisco: Jossey-Bass Inc., 1986), 209-255.

8.Ibid., 228.

9.Ibid., 238.

10.Bruno Bettelheim, *The Use of Enchantment,* cited in Laurent Daloz, 17.

11.Edward Sellner, "Adult Conversion and the Ministry of Sponsor," *Finding and Forming Sponsors and Godparents,* ed. James Wilde (Chicago: Liturgy Training Publications, 1988), 31.

12.*Alcoholics Anonymous Comes of Age* (New York: A.A. World Services, 1957), 79.

13.Gregory M. Smith, *The Fire in their Eyes: Spiritual Mentors for the Christian Life* (New York: Paulist Press, 1984), 39.

14.Clarence Jordan, *The Cotton Patch Version of Matthew and John* (New York: Association Press, 1973), 37.

15.Susanne Johnson, *Christian Spiritual Formation in the Church and Classroom* (Nashville: Abingdon Press, 1989), 21.

16.Francis Kelly Nemeck and Marie T. Coombs, *The Way of Spiritual Direction* (Wilmington, DE: Glazier, Inc., 1989), 44.

17.Stanley Hauerwas and William H. Willimon, *Resident Aliens* (Nashville: Abingdon Press, 1989), 48.

18.Thomas N. Finger, *Christian Theology*, Vol II (Scottdale, PA: Herald Press, 1989), 210.

19.Johnson, 104.

20.David Watson, *Accountable Discipleship* (Nashville: Discipleship Resources, 1986), 33.

21.Dietrich Bonhoeffer, *The Cost of Discipleship*, 2nd ed. (New York: Macmillan, 1963), 93.

22.Ray Anderson, *On Being Human* (Grand Rapids: Eerdmans, 1982), 31.

23.Alan Kreider, *Journey Toward Holiness* (Scottdale, PA: Herald Press, 1987), 38.

24.Kenneth Leech, *Experiencing God* (San Francisco: Harper & Row, 1985), 42.

25.James Fenhagen, *Invitation to Holiness* (San Francisco: Harper & Row, 1985), 18.

26.Anderson, 31.

27.M. Scott Peck, *A Different Drum* (New York: Simon & Schuster, 1987), 68.

28.Thomas Merton, *Life and Holiness* (New York: Image Books, 1964), 21.

29.Ibid., 30.

30.Ibid., 30.

31.Dallas Willard, *The Spirit of the Disciplines* (San Francisco: Harper & Row, 1988), 228.

32.Robert Fabing, *Experiencing God in Daily Life* (Phoenix: Epoch Universal Pub., 1991), 26.

33.John Wesley, "Preface to Hymns and Sacred Poems" (1739), in his *Works*, XIV, 321, quoted by Howard Snyder, *The Radical Wesley* (Downers Grove, IL: InterVarsity Press, 1980), 88.

34.Kenneth R. Davis, *Anabaptism and Asceticism* (Scottdale, PA: Herald Press, 1974), 140.

35.Ibid., 201, 296.

36.Walter Klaassen, ed., *Anabaptism in Outline, Classics of the Radical Reformation*, No 3 (Kitchener, ON: Herald Press, 1984), 23.

37. Davis, 51; see also John R. Martin, *Ventures in Discipleship* (Scottdale, PA: Herald Press, 1984), 273.

38.James Fowler, *Stages of Faith* (San Francisco: Harper & Row, 1981), 287.

39.Loughlan Sofield and Carroll Juliano, *Collaborative Ministry* (Notre Dame, IN: Ave Maria Press, 1987), 60.

40.Finger, *Christian Theology*, Vol. 2 , 260.

41.Kenneth Leech, *Soul Friend* (San Francisco: Harper & Row, 1977), 191.

42.Hans Urs von Balthasar, *Prayer* (San Francisco: Ignatius Press, 1986), 169.

43.Nemeck and Coombs, 95.

44.Ibid., 63.

45.Basil Pennington, *O Holy Mountain* (Garden City, NY: Doubleday, 1978), 255.

46.Frederick Beuchner, *The Alphabet of Grace* (New York: Seabury, 1970), 34.

47.C. S. Lewis, *The Four Loves* (New York: Harcourt, Brace, Jovanovich, 1960), 126.

48.Thomas Merton, *Seven Story Mountain* (New York: Harcourt, Brace, Jovanovich, 1948), 352-356.

49.Dietrich Bonhoeffer, *Spiritual Care* (Philadelphia: Fortress Press, 1985), 64.

50.Cited in Dallas Willard, *The Spirit of the Disciplines* (San Francisco: Harper & Row, 1988), 115.

51.Ibid., 68.

52.Bonhoeffer, *Spiritual Care*, 39.

53.Gerald G. May, *Will and Spirit:A Contemplative Psychology* (San Francisco: Harper and Row, 1982), 297.

54.Andrew Purves, *The Search for Compassion* (Louisville, KY: Westminster/John Knox Press, 1989), 127, 128.

55.Ibid., 132.

56.Johnson, 83.

57.RCIA, 14.

58.For a different viewpoint, see John Driver, *Understanding the Atonement for the Mission of the Church* (Scottdale, PA: Herald Press, 1986), 144.

59.von Balthasar, *Prayer*, 46.

60.Madonna Kolbenschlag, *Lost in the Land of Oz* (San Francisco: Harper and Row, 1988), 9.

61.F. F. Bruce, *The Hard Sayings of Jesus* (Downers Grove, IL: InterVarsity Press, 1983), 24.

62.RCIA, 78.

63.RCIA, 78.

64.Pennington, 176.

65.Scott Peck, *The Road Less Traveled*, 7.

66.John Bradshaw, *The Family* (Deerfield Beach, FL: Health Communications, Inc., 1988), 6.

67.Dorothee Soelle, *Suffering* (Philadelphia: Fortress Press, 1975), 41.

68.*Mennonite Encyclopedia*, Vol V (Scottdale, PA: Herald Press, 1990), 862.

69.Purves, 99.

70.Bonhoeffer, *Spiritual Care*, 52.

71.Ibid., 31.

72.Kilian McDonnell and George Montague, *Christian Initiation and Baptism in the Holy Spirit* (Collegeville, MN: The Liturgical Press, 1991), 307.

73.James Dunn, *Baptism in the Holy Spirit* (Naperville, IL: Alec R. Allenson, Inc., 1970), 5.

74.Lawrence J. Martin, *Living the Baptismal Life* (Scottdale, PA: Mennonite Publishing House, 1990), 77.

75.I. H. Marshall, *I Peter* (Downers Grove, IL: InterVarsity Press, 1991), 130.

76.Davis, 206.

77.Paul M. Lederach, *A Third Way* (Scottdale, PA: Herald Press, 1980), 81.

78.*Baptism, Eucharist and Ministry*, Faith and Order paper, No. 111 (Geneva: World Council of Churches, 1982), Lutheran Edition, 10.

79.Robert Webber, *Liturgical Evangelism* (Harrisburg, PA: Morehouse Pub., 1986), 89-93.

80.RCIA, 115-150.

81.See J. Lawrence Martin, 81-88; and J. Lawrence Martin, *Making Disciples* (Scottdale, PA: Mennonite Publishing House, 1992), 71-91.

BIBLIOGRAPHY

Anderson, Ray S. *On Being Human*. Grand Rapids, MI: Eerdmans, 1982.

Armour, Rollin. *Anabaptist Baptism*. Scottdale, PA: Herald Press, 1966.

Au, Wilkie, S.J. *By Way of the Heart*. New York, N.Y: Paulist Press, 1989.

Banks, Robert. *Paul's Idea of Community*. Grand Rapids, MI: William B. Eerdmans, 1980.

Barth, Karl. *Church Dogmatics*. Vol. IV, trans. G.W. Bromiley. Edinburgh: T.& T. Clark, 1958.

------ *The Teaching of the Church Regarding Baptism*. London: SCM Press, 1954.

Bishops' Committee on the Liturgy. Rite of Christian *Initiation of Adults*. Chicago, IL: Liturgy Training Publications, 1988.

Boers, Arthur P. *On Earth as in Heaven*. Scottdale, PA: Herald Press, 1991.

Bonhoeffer, Dietrich. *The Cost of Discipleship*. New York, NY: The Macmillan Company, 1963.

----- *Life Together*. New York, NY: Harper & Row, 1954.

----- *Meditating On The Word*. Cambridge, MA: Cowley Pub., 1986.

----- *Spiritual Care*. Philadelphia, PA: Fortress, 1985.

Bosch, David J. *A Spirituality of the Road*. Scottdale, PA: Herald Press, 1979.

Boyer, Ernest Jr. *A Way in the World*. San Francisco, CA: Harper & Row, 1984.

Bradshaw, John. *The Family*. Deerfield Beach, FL: Health Communications, Inc., 1988.

Beuchner, Frederich. *The Alphabet of Grace*. New York, NY: Seabury, 1970.

Chittister, Joan, OSB. *Wisdom Distilled from the Daily*. San Francisco, CA: Harper & Row, 1991.

Coles, Robert. *The Spiritual Life of Children*. Boston, MA: Houghton Mifflin, 1990.

Corey, Marianne and Gerald. *Groups: Process and Practice*. 3rd ed., Pacific Grove, CA: Brooks/Cole Publishing, 1987.

Daloz, Laurent. *Effective Teaching and Mentoring*. San Francisco: Jossy-Bass Pub., 1989.

Davis, Kenneth R. *Anabaptism and Asceticism*. Scottdale, PA:Herald Press, 1974.

Driver, John. *Understanding the Atonement*. Scottdale, PA: Herald Press, 1986.

Duggan, Robert and Maureen Kelly. *The Christian Initiation of Children*. New York, NY: Paulist, 1991.

Dyckman, Katherine and Patrick Carroll. *Inviting the Mystic Supporting the Prophet*. New York, NY: Paulist Press, 1981.

Edwards, Tilden. *Spiritual Friend*. New York, NY: Paulist Press, 1980.

Eller, David B., ed. *Servants of the Word*. Elgin, IL: Brethren Press, 1990.

Fabing, Robert, S.J. *Experiencing God In Daily Life*. Phoenix AZ: Epoch Universal Pub., 1991.

Fenhagen, James. *Invitation to Holiness*. San Francisco, CA: Harper & Row, 1985.

Finger, Thomas N. *Christian Theology: an Eschatological Approach*, 2 volumes. Scottdale, PA: Herald Press, 1985-1989.

Fiorenza, Elisabeth. *In Memory of Her*. New York, NY: Crossroad, 1988.

Foster, Richard. *Celebration of Discipline*. New York, NY: Harper & Row, 1978.

------ *Prayer*. San Francisco, CA: Harper & Row, 1992.

Fowler, James. *Becoming Adult, Becoming Christian*. San Francisco, CA: Harper & Row, 1984.

------ *Stages of Faith*. San Francisco, CA: Harper & Row, 1981.

Fretheim, Terence. *The Suffering of God*. Philadelphia, PA: Fortress Press, 1984.

Friedmann, Robert. *Mennonite Piety Through the Centuries*. Scottdale, PA: Herald Press, 1949.

------ *The Theology of Anabaptism*. Scottdale, PA: Herald Press, 1973.

Gibble, June A. and Fred W. Swartz, eds. *Called to Caregiving*. Elgin, IL: Brethren Press, 1987.

Hamilton, Neill Q. *Maturing in the Christian Life*. Philadelphia, PA: The Geneva Press, 1984.

Hauerwas, Stanley. *After Christendom?* Nashville, TN: Abingdon Press, 1991.

Hauerwas, Stanley and William Willimon. *Resident Aliens*. Nashville, TN: Abingdon Press, 1989.

Holifield, Brooks. *A History of Pastoral Care in America*. Nashville, TN: Abingdon Press, 1984.

Hymnal: A Worship Book. Scottdale, PA: Mennonite Publishing House, 1992.

Isabell, Damien. *The Spiritual Director*. Chicago, IL: Franciscan Herald Press, 1976.

Janzen, Susan E., ed. *Making Disciples*. Scottdale, PA: Mennonite Publishing House, 1992.

Jeschke, Marlin. *Believers' Baptism for Children of the Church*. Scottdale, PA: Herald Press, 1983.

Johnson, Ben Campbell. *Pastoral Spirituality*. Philadelphia, PA: The Westminster Press, 1988.

Johnson, Susanne. *Christian Spiritual Formation.* Nashville,TN: Abingdon Press, 1989.

Kanigel, Robert. *Apprentice to Genius.* New York, NY: Macmillan, 1986.

Klassen, Walter, ed. *Anabaptism In Outline.* Scottdale, PA: Herald Press, 1981.

Kreider, Alan. *Journey Toward Holiness.* Scottdale, PA: Herald Press, 1987.

Kolbenschlag, Madonna. *Lost In The Land Of Oz.* San Francisco, CA: Harper & Row, 1988.

Lederach, Paul M. *A Third Way.* Scottdale, PA: Herald Press, 1980.

Leech, Kenneth. *Experiencing God.* San Francisco, CA: Harper & Row, 1985.

----- *Soul Friend.* San Francisco, CA: Harper & Row, 1980.

Lewinski, Ron. *Guide for Sponsors.* Chicago, Il: Liturgy Training Publications, 1987.

Lewis, C.S. *The Four Loves.* New York, NY: Harcourt, Brace, Jovanovich, 1960.

----- *Making Disciples.* Scottdale, PA: Mennonite Publishing House, 1992.

Martin, John. *Ventures in Discipleship.* Scottdale, PA: Herald Press, 1984.

Martin, Lawrence J. *Living the Baptismal Life.* Scottdale, PA: Herald Press, 1992.

May, Gerald. *Care of Mind/Care of Spirit.* San Francisco: Harper & Row, 1982.

McGill, Arthur. *Suffering.* Philadelphia, PA: The Westminster Press, 1982.

McDonnell, Kilian and George Montague. *Christian Initiation and Baptism in the Holy Spirit.* Collegeville, Minn: The Liturgical Press, 1991.

Mckinney, Mary Benet, OSB. *Sharing Wisdom.* Allen, TX: Tabor, 1987.

Mennonite Encyclopedia. Vol V., Scottdale, PA: Herald Press, 1990.

Merton, Thomas. *Contemplative Prayer.* New York, NY: Doubleday, 1969.

------ *Life and Holiness.* New York, NY: Doubleday, 1963.

------ *Seven Story Mountain.* New York, NY: Harcourt Brace, Jovanovich, 1948.

------ *Spiritual Direction and Meditation.* Collegeville, Minn: The Liturgical Press, 1960.

Michael, Chester and Marie Norrisey. *Prayer and Temperament.* Charlottesville, VA: The Open Door, 1991.

Mitchell, Leonel L. *The Meaning of Ritual.* Wilton, CT: Morehouse-Barlow, 1977.

Morris, Thomas H. *Walking Together in Faith.* New York, NY: Paulist Press, 1992.

Miller, Keith J. *A Hunger for Healing.* San Francisco, CA: Harper & Row, 1991.

Nemeck, Francis and Marie Coombs. *The Way of Spiritual Direction.* Wilmington, Delaware: Michael Glazier, 1989.

Nouwen, Henri, Donald McNeill, and Douglass Morrison. *Compassion.* Garden City, NY: Doubleday, 1982.

------ *The Way of the Heart.* New York, NY: Ballantine, 1981.

Oden, Thomas. *Pastoral Theology.* San Francisco, CA: Harper & Row, 1983.

Pannenberg, Wolthart. *Christian Spirituality.* Philadelphia, PA: The Westminster Press, 1983.

Parks, Sharon. *The Critical Years.* San Francisco, CA: Harper & Row, 1986.

Peck, Scott. *The Different Drum.* New York, NY: Simon and Schuster, 1987.

------ *The Road Less Traveled: A New Psychology of Love, Traditional Values, and Spiritual Growth.* New York, NY: Simon and Schuster, 1978.

Pennington, Basil. *O Holy Mountain.* Garden City, N.Y: Doubleday, 1978.

Peterson. Eugene H. *A Long Obedience in the Same Direction.* Downers Grove, IL: Intervarsity Press, 1980.

------ *The Contemplative Pastor.* Dallas, TX: Word, 1989.

------ *Working the Angles.* Grand Rapids, MI: Eerdmans, 1986.

Purves, Andrew. *The Search for Compassion.* Louisville, KY: Westminster/John Knox Press, 1989.

------ *Rite of Christian Initiation of Adults.* Study Edition. Chicago, IL: Liturgy Training Publications, 1988.

Rhodes, Lynn. *Co-Creating: A Feminist Vision of Ministry.* Philadelphia, PA: The Westminster Press, 1987.

Schaef, Anne Wilson. *Co-Dependence.* San Francisco, CA: Harper & Row, 1986.

Smith, Gregory M. *The Fire in their Eyes.* New York, NY: Paulist Press, 1984.

Soelle, Dorothee. *Suffering.* Philadelphia, PA: Fortress Press, 1975.

Sofield, Loughlan, and Carroll Juliano. *Collaborative Ministry.* Notre Dame, IN: Ave Maria Press, 1989.

Strege, Merle D. *Baptism and Church, A Believers' Church Vision.* Grand Rapids, MI: Sagamore Books, 1986.

Urs von Balthasar, Hans. *Prayer.* San Francisco, CA: Ignatius Press,1986.

Watson, David L. *Accountable Discipleship.* Nashville, TN: Discipleship Resources, 1986.

Webber, Robert E. *Liturgical Evangelism.* Harrisburg, PA: Morehouse Pub., 1986.

98

————— *Signs of Wonder*. Nashville, TN: Abbott/Martyn, 1992.

Weil, Simone. *Waiting for God.*, trans. Leslie A. Fiedler. New York, NY: Harper & Row, 1951.

Wilde, James A., ed. *Finding and Forming Sponsors and Godparents*. Chicago, IL: Liturgy Training Pub., 1988.

Willard, Dallas. *The Spirit of the Disciplines*. San Francisco, CA: Harper & Row, 1988.

White, James F. *Protestant Worship*. Louisville, KY: Westminster/John Knox Press, 1989.

World Council of Churches. *Baptism, Eucharist and Ministry*, Faith and Order Paper, No. 11. Geneva: World Council of Churches, 1982.

www.ingramcontent.com/pod-product-compliance
Lightning Source LLC
Chambersburg PA
CBHW060418090426
42734CB00011B/2353